YOUTH PARTICIPATORY EVALUATION

JB JOSSEY-BASS

YOUTH PARTICIPATORY EVALUATION

Strategies for Engaging Young People

KIM SABO FLORES

Foreword by Naomi Ortiz

BICENTENNIAL
1807
WILEY
2007
BICENTENNIAL

HV
1431
.F57
2008

Published by Jossey-Bass
A Wiley Imprint
989 Market Street, San Francisco, CA 94103-1741—www.josseybass.com

Wiley Bicentennial logo: Richard J. Pacifico

Jossey-Bass books and products are available through most bookstores. To contact Jossey-Bass directly call our Customer Care Department within the U.S. at 800-956-7739, outside the U.S. at 317-572-3986, or fax 317-572-4002.

Jossey-Bass also publishes its books in a variety of electronic formats. Some content that appears in print may not be available in electronic books.

Library of Congress Cataloging-in-Publication Data

Flores, Kim Sabo, 1969-
   Youth participatory evaluation : strategies for engaging young people / Kim Sabo Flores ; foreword by Naomi Ortiz. — 1st ed.
        p. cm.
   Includes bibliographical references and index.
   ISBN-13: 978-0-7879-8392-5 (pbk.)
1. Youth—Services for—United States—Evaluation.   2. Social work with youth—United States—Evaluation.   3. Social service—United States—Evaluation—Citizen participation.   4. Evaluation—Study and teaching—United States.   5. Youth development—United States. I. Title.
   HV1431.F57   2008
   361.20835'0973—dc22

                                                              2007028785

Printed in the United States of America
FIRST EDITION

PB Printing   10 9 8 7 6 5 4 3 2 1

CONTENTS

PART ONE: FOUNDATIONS OF YOUTH PARTICIPATORY EVALUATION

PART TWO: DESIGNING AND CONDUCTING YOUTH PARTICIPATORY EVALUATION PROJECTS

To all of the youth and staff I have had the privilege to work with. Thank you for allowing me to take chances and create with you.

PREFACE

The dilemma of trying to understand what I do for a living has become a family joke. Every year at Thanksgiving my relatives pass the phone around the room and ask me to explain my job. I launch in with words and phrases like "building environments with youth," "empowerment," "knowledge production," "democracy," "development," "performance," "creativity," and "evaluation." They say things like "That sounds interesting" or "Oh, that's nice, you work with 'troubled' children—you're a therapist" or "So you're a teacher?" I have been doing this "question asking" activity with my family for the past two decades, and I think we would all agree I have gotten no closer to answering the question for them. What's fascinating about this tradition is that my family persists in asking and I persist in answering. Somehow I have managed to pique their interest while completely confusing them—ah, the postmodern dilemma!

Americans are inquisitive people. We traditionally ask someone we meet for the first time what he or she does for a living. What we are really asking is that the person summarize his or her life in a way that is brief and definitive and gives us a position or role that we can easily understand. The appropriate response to this question is typically something like "I'm a doctor" (or a lawyer or a secretary or an investment banker). However, like many others in this postmodern era, I find this question challenging, and I struggle to come up with an intelligent response.

I hope this book will finally provide clarity for my family and others seeking to understand the emerging field of youth participatory evaluation (YPE) and how it relates to human, organizational, programmatic, social, and community development. *Youth Participatory Evaluation: A Performatory Approach to Evaluation and Youth Development* introduces readers to the benefits of seeing YPE through a developmental lens that highlights the importance of play and performance. It explores a theoretical construct that supports YPE as a developmental activity and provides concrete ways to conduct YPE—in other words, to "play with evaluation." A compendium of activities and approaches gives direction on every step of the YPE process, from preparing adults and youth for projects to research and evaluation methods, data analysis, and report writing. As a whole, the book not only provides a clear picture of how YPE works but also allows practitioners to begin conducting their own YPE projects. While I hope that this book answers many questions, it is also intended to raise many more for readers to grapple with. In the spirit of playful performance, I am more interested in stimulating this dialogic process than in the words that are written here.

■ ■ ■

ACKNOWLEDGMENTS

Thanks to Naomi Ortiz, a brilliant youth evaluator and leader in the field of youth organizing, who at the age of twenty had already begun mentoring me in the skills necessary to become a true collaborator with youth. The lessons she has shared with me have touched me deeply and, I believe, have made me a better person. I am honored that she graciously agreed to write the introduction to this book.

Thank you also to Dr. Anita Baker and Catlin Fullwood, the fabulous women with whom I have collaborated to develop numerous training materials over the years. Several of the activities in this book have been developed in concert with them. Also, I want to thank the Bruner Foundation, the Robert Bowne Foundation, the U.S. Diana Princess of Wales Foundation, and the Cricket Island Foundation for supporting this work and allowing me the time and energy to create.

I feel grateful also to Andy Pasternack for inviting me to write this book and for his tenacity in ensuring that it made its way to publication. Thanks also to the other team members at Jossey-Bass, Muna Farhat and Seth Schwartz, for their valuable practical and scholarly advice. I am also appreciative of the editing support provided by Kathleen Ellis, whose points of clarification and mastery of style helped make my writing clearer and more precise.

Also a big thank-you to my colleague Sarah Zeller-Berkman for the background work she did for this book and her bright, available mind throughout my writing process. I am also deeply grateful to Dr. Roger Hart for ongoing support of my work. It was Roger's suggestion that I explore and help develop the field of youth participatory evaluation in the first place.

I thank my dear friend and mentor Dr. Lois Holzman for helping me conceptualize and realize this book. Her long challenging conversations and critical eye were enormously helpful throughout the writing process. Lois, thank you for "directing" me in my writing and life performances.

Finally, I am thankful to my husband, Jesse Flores, for all of his love, support, and companionship during our many late-night writing sessions at the coffee shop. His ability to listen and question has proved extremely valuable to my writing process.

July 2007   Kim Sabo Flores

THE AUTHOR

Kim Sabo Flores is a seasoned evaluation consultant and leader in the emerging field of youth participatory evaluation. Drawing on her training in developmental and environmental psychology, Flores introduces hundreds of adults and young people, their programs, and their communities to the empowering impact of creative and sustained participation, reflection, and evaluation. In addition, she has worked with numerous foundations to help build their evaluation capacities, supporting them to measure their community impacts and progress toward achieving their missions. Her unique approach highlights the performatory nature of participatory evaluation and the contribution of performance to human learning and development. As founder and principal of Kim Sabo Consulting, Flores generates collaborative projects that educate not only program staff but also their funders about ways that participatory evaluation can help build organizational capacity.

FOREWORD

I met Kim Sabo Flores when I was twenty and serving as the board of directors' cochair of a national youth-run project for young people with disabilities. We were (and still are) dedicated to guaranteeing young people with disabilities a voice in everything that affects us. When I met Kim, we were in the middle of an "organizational development" process, which meant figuring out what the project does, how it works, and why it works. When we were told that we were expected to come up with an evaluation plan, it seemed overwhelming. I was particularly resistant. To me, as a disabled young person, evaluation meant that an adult (usually nondisabled) made a judgment about what kind of classroom I could be in, what kind of say I could have in the care of my body, and even the extent of my participation in the community. Evaluation represented power over every element of my life, as I believe it does for most young people. The turning point that changed my belief about who had the right to say what was working and what was not working in my life came when I became involved in youth participatory evaluation (YPE).

By the time Kim came on board, she had heard of our issues in working with other evaluators to develop a plan for our project. Other evaluators had not grasped what we meant when we said we wanted an "accessible process." They did not understand why having everyone involved, no matter what their disability, was essential. Kim listened to our frustration and then surprised us all by agreeing that she did not have the expertise needed to complete the plan. Instead, she told us that we did!

It took hours for Kim to explain the YPE process to a few of us. Then we translated the language, processes, and activities to make them accessible for our community. As disabled youth, we are often viewed as the most vulnerable, the most "unable" to know what we need. To have a nondisabled adult tell us that we could be the experts to decide what would work for us was profound. This philosophy shifted my view of adult-youth partnership and, most of all, challenged my ideas on what my role as a cochair of an all-youth board should be. Through this experience, youth board members became more than "leaders." We became responsible for our own community. And we developed an awesome evaluation plan that has served our project for years. The YPE process led to shifts in thinking in both the young people and the staff and has deeply permeated the work we do.

Having youth identify the need, develop the process, and collect information is important for many reasons. Many people have had the experience of being an outsider, a person whose opinion is not valued. For youth, this is often their entire life experience with systems of power. Young people are taught that they are the reason these systems exist: to teach, influence, and condition them to act in certain ways for the good of society. Information and ultimately power are usually presented as beyond the ability of young people to comprehend; they cannot understand the big picture, the overall process of deciding what works and what doesn't, what has value and what doesn't. We were all raised with this belief that the big picture is "beyond us," so we have to trust someone else's understanding of the big picture. When we become adults, it becomes overwhelming to figure out how to be a good citizen and to make decisions about the things that really affect our lives. We are not taught to value our own experience or knowledge.

But what if we were treated as experts of our environments and experiences? What if we were offered tools and guidance to look at the big picture, to collect information that would directly affect our lives? Would our experiences as adults be different? I believe we would be deeply affected. We would be less fearful of the systems put in place to govern our lives. We would feel empowered to make changes based on information we gathered from ourselves and our peers.

Adults who work for social justice are often disappointed by what they describe as the apathy, the uncaring attitude, of voters, neighbors, and citizens. These criticisms are also often placed on youth. However, if we taught young people that their experiences were valued and could lead to change, the ripple effects would be tremendous. Youth participatory evaluation is an approach that can help young people who are used to being treated as "objects" that are studied and manipulated to break free of that passive role and take responsibility for themselves and others, to be seen as a resource.

Kim Sabo Flores has written a book that will be a valuable resource for any evaluator, educator, young person, or adult who wants the world to grow into a better place. Ultimately, it is not the answers to our questions that hold power but the questions themselves. Asking the individuals who are most affected by their own experiences what their questions are regarding their life, their world, or the project they are involved in gives them a chance to present a framework that is authentic, real, and useful as a benchmark against which to measure change. We all crave validation and have hopes for our future. By creating the space for young people to participate in their own evaluation, we can build a vision that will give us all hope.

July 2007   Naomi Ortiz

YOUTH PARTICIPATORY EVALUATION

PART

1

FOUNDATIONS OF YOUTH PARTICIPATORY EVALUATION

Part One of this book explores the foundations of youth participatory evaluation, including the definition of YPE and its history, principles, and benefits. It also highlights the significance of Vygotsky's developmental theory in YPE. Chapter One introduces youth participatory

1

evaluation to newcomers to the field and provides a consolidated overview for those who have some familiarity with it. Chapter Two addresses the questions of why and how YPE contributes to the development of youth, programs, organizations, adults, communities, and evaluation itself. It also provides a theoretical construct that helps account for these diverse outcomes.

CHAPTER

1

AN INTRODUCTION TO YOUTH PARTICIPATORY EVALUATION

When you have finished reading this chapter, you will know more about the following:

- The history of youth participatory evaluation (YPE) and how it has emerged out of the philosophies and tenets of both positive youth development and participatory evaluation

- What YPE is

- How other professionals have been thinking about youth participation in evaluation and research

- How YPE supports youth, adult, program, and community development

- How YPE can and should support development in evaluation

Youth participatory evaluation involves young people in the process of evaluating the programs, organizations, agencies, and systems that have been designed to serve them. The YPE process can be completely youth-driven, or it can be conducted in partnership with adults. In either case, the youth in YPE projects are provided with support to perform as evaluators. They are not merely respondents of methods created by adults, nor are they consultants on adult-led evaluations. Instead, they are the creators of knowledge, shaping their own evaluation questions, developing their own unique methods, analyzing and interpreting the data gathered, and reporting their findings.

I began my search for youth participatory evaluation in 1995. At the time I was a graduate student working at the Children's Environments Research Group (CERG). My colleagues and I were studying children's participation in research, environmental planning, and social change. Because of our group's expertise in the field of children's participation, we were asked to become part of a California Wellness Foundation initiative to improve children's environments throughout California. I was asked to find examples of youth involvement in program evaluations. This seemed easy enough. After all, we were living in very exciting times for the field of youth and child participation. Many research projects were examining the impacts of youth participation in decision making, governance, research, planning, and design. Theorists were writing about the effects of participation on youth development, and social and political theorists were positing the benefits of youth participation on community and social development.

A catalyst for all of this activity was the signing and ratification of the International Convention on the Rights of the Child, which in Articles 12 through 15 recognizes children's participation as a fundamental right. This understanding of children as full citizens with rights and responsibilities led many countries to experiment with youth participation in local government (such as town councils), urban planning, environmental education and justice, and program development.

These practices were built on new research findings that highlighted the importance of positive youth development. At this time social scientists were discovering that while preventing high-risk behaviors was surely a good thing, it was not necessarily developmental for youth. In other words, even those adolescents who attended school, obeyed laws, and avoided drugs were not necessarily equipped to meet the difficult demands of adulthood (Sabo, 1999). This body of research emphasized the need to move from a preventive mind-set toward a developmental one—from thinking that *youth problems are the principal barrier to youth development* to *valuing youth development as the most effective strategy for the prevention of youth problems* (Pittman & Wright, 1991). Youth began to be viewed as assets and resources in communities rather than as delinquents who were feared and whose behaviors needed to be modified or prevented. This new understanding of young people fostered experimentation with a variety of new strategies and methodologies that developed youth leadership and agency (Camino & Zeldin, 1999), related to youth as community builders (Checkoway & Finn, 1992), and empowered youth to become social change agents, community organizers, and activists (Camino, 1992; James & McGillicuddy, 2001).

It was in this rich climate of experimentation and change that I found myself searching for models of youth participation in evaluation. I soon discovered an emerging field called participatory evaluation. Participatory evaluation is a type of evaluation that calls for the inclusion of stakeholders, that is, anyone with a vested interest in the evaluation process. However, I found that both the type and level of stakeholder involvement varied greatly from project to project, depending on the needs of the client and the philosophical perspective of the evaluation consultant.

Participatory evaluation grew out of two distinct streams of thought and practice. The first, practical participatory evaluation (P-PE), has the goal of making evaluation findings more useful to the programs being evaluated. From this perspective, the participation of stakeholders in the evaluation process is thought to enhance the relevance and ownership of findings, which in turn makes it more likely that evaluation results will be used to support programmatic development (Cousins & Whitmore, 1998). The second stream, transformative participatory evaluation (T-PE), grew out of a desire to support the transformation and empowerment of individuals and groups through the process of constructing and respecting their own knowledge.

While reviewing this literature to find examples of how young people had been involved as stakeholders in these participatory evaluations, I came across a study that had surveyed all members of the American Evaluation Association about their participatory evaluation practices (Cousins, Donohue, & Bloom, 1996). This study identified over five hundred practitioners using some type of participatory process in their evaluation work. Thrilled to find such a comprehensive overview of the field, I called Dr. Cousins, the lead researcher, to ask how many of these projects had been conducted in youth programs, after-school programs, or schools. My assumption was that if participatory evaluations had taken place in these environments, youth would most certainly have been regarded as stakeholders with a vested interest in the growth of the project. Dr. Cousins was extremely helpful and made time to talk with me about his study. After determining that many of the programs in his study served children or youth, I asked Dr. Cousins which evaluations had involved youth in the process. After a long pause he asked, "Do you mean as evaluators?" I said yes. He then told me that not one of the programs had included young people in the process. After an awkward silence, I explained that I thought all stakeholders were supposed to be involved in participatory evaluation. He agreed but couldn't think of any person in the United States or Canada who was actually engaging the largest constituent group—children and youth—in their evaluation projects. I think that he was also a bit shocked by this discovery. He told me that to date, most of the participatory evaluation studies had focused on including staff in the process rather than clients.

I couldn't believe this. I had a million questions: How could it be possible to conduct a participatory evaluation process that included "all stakeholders" without engaging the very people who attended the program? How could we possibly move forward to create programs to meet the needs of young people if we weren't engaging them in the development and evaluation of their programs? If we were to take seriously the tenets of youth development, how could we not engage youth in authentic leadership roles and activities in the programs that served them? And finally, following the tenets of the Convention on the Rights of the Child, how were we to engage youth as citizens if we were not serious about including them in basic, local-level decision making and knowledge production? I was struck by the incongruence of data before me. My perplexity and outrage led to what has now become a more than decadelong journey to discover what it means to engage youth fully in evaluation and knowledge production processes.

WHAT IS YOUTH PARTICIPATORY EVALUATION?

I eventually discovered that I was not the only person asking these questions. After an intensive two-year search in which I reviewed every electronic mailing list, database, Web site, book, magazine, and foundation report that had anything to do with child and youth participation, I found a handful of like-minded colleagues who were doing amazing work engaging children and youth in evaluation processes. Five of these trailblazers allowed me to conduct a study of their programs and projects. Their efforts and the efforts of the young people in these programs became the topic of my doctoral dissertation. What developed out of this research was very important—we became less alone in the world, and we began developing a field of study and practice that became known as youth participatory evaluation.

Over the past seven years, leaders of this emerging field have held three significant meetings at which we collectively explored youth participation and delineated the field for researchers and evaluators. The first meeting, "Children's Participation in Community Settings," took place in 1999 and was sponsored by Childwatch International Research Network and the Growing Up in Cities project of the MOST Programme of UNESCO. In 2000 the second meeting, "Youth Participation in Community Research and Evaluation," was hosted by the Social Work and Urban Planning Department of the School of Social Work at the University of Michigan and supported by the Kellogg Foundation. During the third meeting, a much larger conference with the same name held in Wingspread, Wisconsin, specific strategies for advancing youth participatory evaluation as a new field of practice were discussed. Other significant advances in the field included a *New Directions for Evaluation* volume, *Youth Participatory Evaluation: A Field in the Making,* which marked the first publication devoted entirely to this topic (Sabo, 2003a), and a *CYD Journal: Community Youth Development* edition titled "Youth Participation in Community Evaluation and Research" (Checkoway, Dobbie, & Richards-Schuster, 2003). In addition, *Evaluation Exchange,* the newsletter of the prestigious Harvard Family Research Project, began featuring reports on projects using YPE. These were all significant triumphs for our small but emerging field.

One of the major accomplishments of the 2002 meeting on Youth Participation in Community Research and Evaluation was that participants were able to develop a working definition for the field and a core set of principles to guide our practices (see Exhibit 1.1). The definition created at this meeting states:

> *Youth Participation in community evaluation research involves young people in knowledge development at the community level. The process includes efforts by adults to involve young people in the research or evaluation of public agencies and private institutions; by young people to organize their own research or evaluation projects; and by youth and adults to work together in intergenerational relationships [Checkoway et al., 2003].*

EXHIBIT 1.1. **Wingspread Declaration of Principles for Youth Participation in Community Research and Evaluation.**

- Youth participation in community research and evaluation transforms its participants. It transforms our ways of knowing, the strategies we devise, the methods we employ, and our program of work.

- Youth participation promotes youth empowerment. It recognizes the experience and expertise of all young people and respects their leadership capacities and potential contributions.

- Youth participation builds mutually liberatory partnerships. It values the assets of all ages and fosters supportive and respectful youth-youth and youth-adult working relationships.

- Youth participation equalizes power relationships between youth and adults. It establishes a level playing field, clarifying for participants the purpose of the process and the power in balances between groups. It structures environments that respect the involvement of young people and trains adults in supporting genuine youth decision making and leadership development.

- Youth participation is an inclusive process that recognizes all forms of democratic leadership, young and old. It involves diverse populations and perspectives, especially those who are traditionally underserved and underrepresented.

- Youth participation involves young people in meaningful ways. Young people participate in all stages of the process, from defining the problem to gathering and analyzing the information to making decisions and taking action.

- Youth participation is an ongoing process, not a one-time event. Participants continuously clarify and reflect upon its purpose and content. Research and evaluation are viewed as an integral part of knowledge development, program planning, and community improvement.

Checkoway et al. (2003)

These principles highlight our collective understanding of youth participation in community research and evaluation as transformative and developmental for individuals, programs, organizations, communities, society, and modes of knowing. YPE is defined as inclusive, engaging young people in all levels of the evaluation effort. Beyond that it seeks to build and strengthen relationships among all stakeholders. Finally, it is ongoing and integral to the work of programs.

THE BENEFITS OF YOUTH PARTICIPATORY EVALUATION

For me, it seems that kids really need to own something. Kids don't own anything. They don't have any say about what their families do; they basically don't have very much control over their lives. The way that I look at it is that it would really make me happy if I knew that at least one kid felt as though he or she had some sort of say in this place and had some sort of ownership over what happened in this place because kids, I think, are very alienated from what is happening in their lives, you know? And they are really powerless. That is why I think it is important to participate in the evaluation process.

Beth, age 17, participant in a youth-led drug prevention program in Canada

As the field has grown, so has the literature documenting the impacts of youth participation projects. Specific studies have focused on youth participation in research, governance, and decision making at the programmatic, local community, national, and international policy levels. While this book focuses specifically on youth participation in evaluation, the insights gleaned from these other closely aligned fields are very useful both in theory and in practice.

Numerous recent studies and reports show that youth participation has multiple benefits for young people, adult facilitators, programs, communities, society, and the field of evaluation itself. Although these benefits are interrelated and dynamic, I will first discuss each separately and then explore their connections to one another in the next chapter, "Performance, Play, and Development."

Benefits to Youth

We grew a lot; we experienced a lot. We hung out with our friend and adults and other kids. I think I wouldn't be who I am now if I hadn't worked in this program.

Bob, age 17, member of a YPE team conducted in a youth shelter in Canada

*You develop more mature relationships with adults. I wasn't getting
that before I got involved with this project. Where would you get it?*

Karen, age 15, participant in a youth-led prevention
program in Canada

In the past five years a wide variety of publications have examined
how young people benefit from their involvement in research or evalua-
tion or both (Calvert, Zeldin, & Weisenbach, 2002; Camino, 2001, 2005;
Golombek, 2002; Horsch, Little, Chase Smith, Goodyear, & Harris,
2002; Larson et al., 2003; Lewis-Charp, Yu, & Soukamneuth, 2006;
London, 2000; Sabo, 1999; Sommers, 2001; Zeldin, Larson, Camino, &
O'Connor, 2005; Youth in Focus (2002); Zimmerman & London (2003).
While each of these authors has a unique perspective on the issue,
London et al. (2005) do an excellent job of summarizing the range of
benefits to youth that can be expected:

- Social competencies: Youth learn to interact and handle new situations and develop empathy for other perspectives. Youth participation builds teamwork and a sense of responsibility.

- Civic competencies: Youth learn social, political, and cultural
  conditions and increased social responsibility and civic leadership
  in areas such as communication, outreach, and advocacy.

- Self-confidence: Youth learn skills in public speaking, talking with
  others, and interviewing and gain confidence that they have knowledge and insight.

- Social capital: Youth build new relationships with peers and adults
  in the community. These new connections can help with future opportunities such as programs and employment.

- Identity exploration: Youth take on new roles as researchers, evaluators, and action planners, broadening their perspectives and sense
  of empowerment.

Other researchers have identified additional impacts, including these:

- Youth learn about knowledge production (Lewis-Charp et al., 2006).

- Youth become more reflective about themselves and their contexts (Hart, 1997).

- Youth develop job readiness skills (London, Zimmerman, & Erbstein, 2003; Sabo, 1999).

- Youth feel personal satisfaction and enjoyment (Sabo, 1999).

Youth participatory evaluation and research projects are conducted in particular types of organizations with varying management and decision-making structures. These projects are facilitated by a diverse array of adults who bring their own sets of values, beliefs, and practices to the work, and they engage a wide range of young people of different ages and capabilities from different social, political, and cultural backgrounds. These contexts can either support or limit certain levels of participation or political involvement. For example, some projects might offer opportunities for young people to be involved in higher-level programmatic, organizational, community, or national decision making.

BECOMING A YOUTH EVALUATOR In 2001

I was fortunate to work with a terrific youth-led organization based in Chicago. One of the young leaders of this program came to love evaluation and made it her mission to learn all she could about the process. Not only did she run training sessions for other young people in her program, but she also helped other young people become evaluators in their own programs. When I asked her how she thought she had benefited by participating in evaluation processes, she said, "The whole process was very intimidating at first. This was on a totally different level of learning than what you do at school—there you learn information. With this you identify important information and effectively put it into use. It has been challenging, but I feel so much more prepared for my future in the working world because of the skills I have gained. You feel a great sense of accomplishment."

Benefits to Adults

A growing body of research mentions the importance of adult development through adult-youth partnerships (Calvert et al., 2002; Camino, 2001, 2005; London, 2000, 2002). In one study on youth participation in governance (Zeldin, 2004), the author found that the majority of adults who were involved in these projects received benefits from partnering with youth in organizational decision making. She found that these partnerships enhanced adults' sense of personal efficacy and belonging. The process of working with youth made adults feel as if they could "better understand the concerns, language and perspectives of contemporary youth, and as a result, they felt that they were making better decisions as well as making them with increased confidence" (p. 86). Sharing successes with youth exhilarated most of the adults, reinforced collective purposes, and led to increased feelings of organizational membership and commitment. The study also noted that adults acted more responsibly with youth at the table.

Others have argued that adult development is needed as a precursor to adult-youth partnerships and should be a focus of professional development (London, 2002). Adult development in this sense implies increasing facilitative leadership skills in which adults are trained to let go of authority while still offering young people the support they need to succeed. Building adults' capacity to help means teaching them skills in active listening, cultural competency, community knowledge, and recognizing varying youth skills (London, 2002).

Benefits to Programs and Organizations That Serve Youth

The juvenile justice system needs to change. Kids go and get locked up and they get back out and they go right back again. It is like a setup to me. It doesn't need to be like that. They need to be helping these youth to get skills so that they can go and get jobs, so they don't have to go back, so they don't have to go back on the streets, to put themselves at risk. So that is why I was interested in this evaluation, 'cause I know a lot of people that have been [harmed] in the juvenile justice system and I'd rather see a change.

Monica, age 17, working on a YPE project that evaluated the
juvenile justice system in San Francisco

Even though all of the young women here have been in the same situations, we are different now. We are employed; we are linked to systems of care. We're disconnected from those youth on the street now. I'm separated; no matter how much I go out onto the streets, it is not the same. So getting information, not just by word of mouth but on paper from the young women who we are serving, is critical so we can improve our program.

Shaniqua, age 19, working in a youth-run prevention
program in California

One of the primary advantages of youth participation in evaluation is to gain their perspectives in order to develop and improve the programs serving them. When young people are involved in the process of evaluation, they can use the data to change their programs according to their needs. The impact of adult-youth partnerships in evaluation and research can reverberate to transform the cultures of entire programs and organizations (Horsch et al., 2002; Kirshner, O'Donoghue, & McLaughlin, 2002; London, 2002; Senge, 1990; Wheeler, 2000; Zeldin, 2004; Zeldin et al., 2005). According to Sommers (2001), if youth are "left out of the process of evaluating the implementations and outcomes of programs that have an impact on their lives, attempts to empower youth may be overshadowed or undermined by the very activities that are meant to empower them" (p. 31). Thus the activity of engaging youth in the evaluation process is more than a means of improving the quality of the data or ensuring that particular constituencies are heard; it is a process that both mirrors and supports the tenets of positive youth development and leads to stronger and more appropriate programming.

Many of the staff members and young people I have worked with over the years have used the YPE process as a starting point for overall programmatic reform. They found that engaging youth in evaluation processes have actually bolstered the level of youth participation in their programs and helped initiate youth participation in ongoing programmatic decision making. When the principles and practices of YPE became embedded and sustained in the organizational structures, programs became more democratic and inclusive of young people's views, perspectives, and power. To make this radical move, programs flattened their hierarchical structures and developed systems that support true participation, reflection, and feedback.

INCREASING PARTICIPATION OF YOUTH USING YPE
In 2001 as a part of a U.S. Diana Princess of Wales initiative, I was asked to lead a YPE team to help conduct an evaluation of a youth theater program. The young people in this program were very much involved in mounting a variety of performances every year, helping with the writing of scripts, acting, singing, dancing, directing, and participating in other ways. However, when it came to actual organizational decision making, only one or two key young people were included.

When the YPE team began our evaluation process, we met with a wide range of youth participants. During our meetings we explored the many questions they had about their program. We were particularly

---

The Impact of YPE on Communities and Society

The longer you stick with it, the greater the public awareness. I've definitely noticed a difference, and it may just be that I'm getting older, but I think that it is also that as you become involved in your community, you are seen in a different light. Like business owners being nicer. I remember one week going into a store and being asked to leave for not being eighteen—and I hadn't done anything. I came back a week later and the owner was like "Oh, hi, sweetheart, I saw your picture in the paper."

Mary, age 18, working in a youth-run program in a rural
town in Canada

In the past several decades, young people have been involved in using community-based action research and evaluation for activism and advocacy. While not every youth participatory evaluation or research project results in community or societal change, many do support young people to develop bodies of knowledge that can be used to bring about changes in communities—schools, families, towns. Research demonstrates that when youth are encouraged and supported to become actively involved in changing issues, programs, and institutions that affect their lives, they have the potential to alter societal structures (Ginwright & James, 2002; Heath, 2000).

The impact of YPE on society comes at the intersection of youth development, youth research, and youth civic engagement. Through

interested in how they, as youth participants, felt about a program that was led by adults. After conducting multiple interviews and focus groups, the YPE team discovered that most of the young people wanted and felt it necessary to become more involved in programmatic decision making. Using our evaluation process as an example of the type of participation they desired, the young people began advocating for greater youth involvement. By the end of our work together, several youth committees had been formed and the adult staff members had started experimenting with a variety of ways to bring more young people into the program as paid staff and members of the board of directors.

participatory evaluation and research projects, young people often have opportunities to become civically involved. This type of engagement often differs from more traditional "civic engagement" and "civic leadership" projects in that young people are immediately involved as full citizens—collecting data, advocating, rallying, organizing peers, holding public hearings, meeting officials, and conducting press conferences. In other words, youth research and evaluation engages youth in civic development through direct action (Sherrod, Flanagan, & Youniss, 2002; Youniss et al. 2002). YPE is in many ways an answer to the call by civic scholars for youth to be given "not just knowledge but also opportunities for participation and practice" (Sherrod et al., 2002, p. 269).

YPE has also been seen as one way to deal with the adult-youth power differential because knowledge production is a form of power (James, 2001). Giving youth the opportunities to produce knowledge reshapes these power dynamics. The activity of empowering young people to have a voice in society can ultimately transform society, creating new roles for both young people and adults.

YPE'S EFFECT ON CITYWIDE POLICY RE-FORM Early in my search for evaluation projects that involved young people, I found the work of Coleman Advocates and their youth program Y-MAC (Youth Making a Change), located in San Francisco. At that time, Y-MAC had just completed an intensive evaluation of all

city-funded agencies serving youth in the Bay Area. Their objective was to understand the extent to which these agencies were actually meeting the needs of young people. Together, Coleman staff and Y-MAC youth developed a "report card" that listed multiple indicators of success. Young people were trained to use the report card as an assessment tool and were sent into each of the programs as undercover evaluators. To develop report cards for each of the agencies, the young people brought the data together to analyze. Once they were certain of their findings, they called each of the agencies and told them about the project. Y-MAC undercover youth evaluators then invited each agency to meet with them to discuss their program assessments from the youth participants' perspective. The young people assured the program directors that their efforts were conducted for the sole purpose of improving the programs. This project was used to advocate for young people to be on the city planning and evaluation committee for all youth-supported programs in San Francisco. In this way, youth were able to transform not only their individual programs but also the means by which the city planned and evaluated the success of all youth programs.

Benefits of YPE on Evaluation

Youth participatory evaluation holds the potential to be a launching point of democratic dialogue. At a time when expert, technical knowledge predominates over knowledge derived from everyday experience and active citizenship, new strategies are needed to allow traditionally underrepresented groups to develop their knowledge resources as part of the broader movement for democratization. This has the potential to break the monopoly of knowledge development and enable young people to gain knowledge and skills for active participation in a democratic society (Checkoway et al., 2003).

Researchers and practitioners have discussed the wonderfully rich and creative methods youth develop when they are involved in evaluation efforts. They have noted that youth are often more capable of obtaining relevant data from other youth than adults are. But few have examined the fundamental shift that evaluation needs to take when it engages young people. Some challenge the field of evaluation to truly engage both young people and all of humanity in the process of continuously creating evaluation, not just by following the methodological rules set forth by the academy but by engaging in critical dialogue that challenges the tenets of the field.

I have long suggested that the merger of youth development and evaluation requires a significant paradigm shift (see Sabo, 2003b). Such a shift has the potential to revise the very nature of what it means to "evaluate":

> *Youth development theorists and practitioners are not concerned with the empirical production of knowledge in the same way that evaluation practitioners are. Instead, they are interested in creating leaders, citizens, social-change agents, community organizers, and healthy youth. The fundamental paradigm shift that development brings to bear on evaluation moves the field away from the question of "how do we engage youth in knowledge production?" to "how do we produce environments that support ongoing growth and change? [p. 8].*

YPE: CHANGING THE WAY EVALUATION IS DONE

In 2001 I was asked to work with a youth-run organization that served young people with disabilities. This group had already hired and fired several exceptionally worthy consultants whom I respected for their ability to facilitate high levels of quality youth participation. I was terrified to work with these young people! During one of our first conference calls, the young people told me that the previous consultants had not really taken their specific needs into consideration when delivering assistance and training. These consultants, I was told, just "didn't understand them." I took this to mean that the previous consultants weren't making an effort to learn more about this group and its unique set of needs. I doubted I could do better, but I remained on the phone and listened. At the end of our first conversation, the young people asked me, "So what do you need from us?" I responded as openly and candidly as I could so that they could come to know me and my own fears and anxieties. "I want you not to fire me," I said. We all laughed, and then I added, "No, really, I'm serious. I want to do whatever it takes for you not to fire me, and I think I'm going to need your help." This moment became the basis for the rest of our work together, work that required all of our honesty, trust, and commitment to the process.

On a freezing-cold day in Chicago I finally met with a key group of the leaders from the program. This meeting preceded an evaluation training session I was to conduct with all of the youth board members. I was eager to learn everything I could about the young people so that I could better conduct the training. About three hours into the meeting it became painfully clear to me that all of the techniques I typically use with youth just wouldn't work with this group. Due to a variety of physical disabilities, many of the young people couldn't move around the room; some couldn't even raise their hand. Many others, I was told, wouldn't be able to understand the materials I had brought with me. Out of frustration, I finally said, "It would be easier for you to learn everything I know about evaluation than it would for me to learn everything you know about the youth in your program." At first we all laughed, but it quickly became clear that this was indeed a better approach. The depth of knowledge it would take to fully understand the range of disabilities represented in the group would take me years to understand. On the other hand, these youth were experts at negotiating all the physical and mental needs of the group, and they were certainly capable of learning evaluation strategies.

We stayed up most of that night preparing. The young people asked me again and again for clarification of particular definitions of terms such as *inputs, activities, outcomes*, and *indicators*. After defining each term, one young person said, "Why don't you just say what you mean? Why do you have to use those words?" I thought about it and realized how right she was. Why *was* I using those words? Had my academic training taken over completely? Had I become so narrow in my thinking that I was actually unable to see there were other much simpler ways of talking about and practicing evaluation? In the end *inputs* became "what you need," *activities* became "what you do," *outcomes* became "what happens," and *indicators* became "what you see."

The next morning these young people held the most dynamic and successful evaluation training I had ever seen. As I watched them transform my understanding of evaluation into something else, something unique, something actually understandable, it made me question all of my practices, whether with young people or adults. To this day, I bring the experience of working with this group with me wherever I go.

CHAPTER

2

DEVELOPMENT, PLAY, AND PERFORMANCE

When you have finished reading this chapter, you will know more about the following:

- How YPE fosters youth, adult, program, and community development

- Vygotsky's developmental theories and how they can be used as a framework for understanding and practicing YPE

- The importance of collectively creating environments that support and sustain ongoing human development

- The significance of performance and creativity in the creation of developmental environments

- How YPE can support the ongoing creation of suitable developmental environments

My two-year research project not only put me in contact with colleagues who were doing exciting work with young people in evaluation but also gave me the opportunity to study what they were doing in detail. I discovered that young people in these types of projects were being supported to perform in new and very different types of roles, as interviewers, reporters, researchers, mentors, leaders, and public speakers, among many others. Young people's assets were not merely being identified and built on as we understand from youth development literature; rather, groups were collectively creating opportunities to explore entirely new ways of being in the world. Through their interactions with one another, both adult facilitators and youth were creating new roles, new attitudes, and new actions. All participants, including the adults, were trying out new things, publicly making mistakes and admitting to them, laughing, joking, and having fun.

As I observed these programs, something seemed unique yet very familiar. The one place where I had experienced a similar level of ensemble creativity was in the theater. As a former actor, I understood the importance of working together with others to create a play, an improvisation, a show. I also valued the ways in which performance could help young people and adults develop as human beings. From experience, I had come to believe that performance was the centerpiece of my own development as a young woman and later as an adult. It was through performance that I was able to *try on* and create a vast array of identities, life histories, costumes, emotions, genders, ethnicities, and classes. This form of play allowed me to stretch myself, to see what I would not otherwise have seen, to be who I would not otherwise have chosen to be, to remove my own moral imperatives in order to understand and perform as *the other*. In the theater, this type of performatory play does not happen in a vacuum, nor does it spring from one person alone. It happens in groups, in interaction with other performers, on a stage for all to see. Any actor will tell you that performance is a fundamentally social endeavor, requiring an ensemble—people to provide feedback and to build and create with. Performance also requires an audience, as it is in the interaction between performer and audience where the true play actually occurs.

What I was observing in these youth participatory evaluation projects was very much like participating in a theater group. In these programs and projects, young people and adults were creating environments in which play and performance were integral to the evaluation work and to the development of all of the participants. Over the years I have come to believe that there is much to be learned about these unique environments. There is a freedom to play and create that is rare in most other environments. Time and time again, both youth and adults have told me that their experiences in these types of playful, performatory environments are transformative.

I am not alone in making such discoveries about performance and play. Reporting on her study of highly effective youth organizations, Shirley Brice Heath (2000) finds that *role playing* is central to the effectiveness of the program. She documents the numerous and varied opportunities for young people to perform in new and different types of roles. She found that as young people performed, they came to see themselves as "capable of acting outside and beyond the expected" (p. 39).

Heath also examines the critical role that adults and peers play in these contexts—often as "audience members" and "ensemble" cast members. Heath (2000) identifies the fundamentally dialectical and social nature of performance, stating that "a sense of self-identity and of the projected self never lie entirely 'within,' but always in the dialectical constructions of how one appears to others" (p. 38). Heath continues this line of reasoning and builds a link between performance characteristics and human development:

> Each individual learns to become human by doing what others already do, in incorporating this general model, each "plays," at different times and in multiple ways, a wide range of roles. It is, therefore, difficult to assume roles one has never witnessed: verbal explication and demonstration by a caring respected adult or older peer help make this possible [p. 38].

The fundamentally dialectical and social nature of human development and its link to performance and play was also the key focus of Lev Vygotsky's work in the early 1900s. Vygotsky, a Marxist psychologist, viewed development as a participatory and relational activity. As he understood it, development was not something that occurred within an individual child (as has been the traditional understanding) but was the relationship between what a child could do independently and what a child could do in collaboration with others. He termed this relational activity the *zone of proximal development* (ZPD), emphasizing that we as human beings are not merely who we are at any given moment but simultaneously who we are and who we are becoming through our interactions with others. Although Vygotsky never actually defined the ZPD, he offered the following description:

> Every function in the child's cultural development appears twice: first on the social level and later on the individual level; first between people (interpsychological), and then inside the child (intrapsychological). This applies equally to all voluntary attention, to logical memory, and

*to the formation of concepts. All the higher mental functions origi-
nate as actual relations between people [1978, p. 57].*

What happens in the ZPD has many similarities to what happens during play and performance; we are able to go beyond ourselves to do what we do not yet know how to do, stretching ourselves and our identities. As Vygotsky puts it, children learn and develop by "performing a head taller than they are" (1978, p. 102), which is the very essence of human growth and development.

Vygotsky articulated two specific activities that dominate the creation of zones of proximal development: *creative imitation* and being related to *as*. Creative imitation allows young people to do what they are not yet capable of. In this sense, imitation is not the "rote imitation of mimicry of the parrot, but an imitation that produces something new, a developmental, creative imitation" (Holzman, 1995, p. 8). We see this type of creative imitation often with very young children. For instance, think about how children play house, performing the roles of mommy and daddy. They are not actually mommy and daddy, but they are creatively imitating the behavior and simultaneously making the roles their own. As Newman and Holzman (1993) state:

> *When children, for example, play Mommy and Daddy they are least like Mommy and Daddy because Mommy and Daddy are not playing or performing; they are acting out their societally predetermined roles. We are all cast by society into very sharply determined roles; what one does in a role is act it. Performance differs from acting in that it is the socialized activity of people self-consciously creating new roles out of what exists for a social performance. Children playing Mommy and Daddy are not acting but performing—creating new roles for themselves, reorganizing environmental scenes. In this sense, "zpd play" is a history game—the putting together of elements of the social environment in ways which help to see and show meaning-making as creative, productive activity—which produces learning-leading-development [pp. 102–103].*

But what does "learning-leading-development" mean? Vygotsky saw learning and development not as separate functions but as a dialectic unity. Using Marx's dialectical historical materialism as a new conceptual tool, Vygotsky was introducing to psychology a new conception of change—change as qualitative transformation of *totalities* (Holzman, 1997). From this viewpoint, learning, instruction, and development are inextricably connected. Vygotsky was not merely identifying another way that learning/instruction and development are related. Rather, he introduced to psychology a new concept of relationship itself, one not premised on *particulars* but on *totalities*" (Holzman, 1997, p. 57).

The second component of creating a ZPD is being related or treated *as*: *as* your performance, *as* your role, *as* who you are becoming. This little word *as* highlights the very social and dialectical nature of development. In other words, it is important for the other to see and relate to you *as* rather than *as if*. The distinction between *as* and *as if* is subtle yet extremely powerful. For example, imagine going to the theater and watching the actors perform *as if* they were their characters. We would have a very different experience, one in which we might not be able to suspend our disbelief sufficiently to involve ourselves fully in the production. Young people and adults also need audiences and "cast members" (or team members) who see and relate to them *as*. In the case of youth participatory evaluation projects, young people need to be understood and related to *as* evaluators, not merely *as if* they were evaluators.

PERFORMING A HEAD TALLER I once worked on

a project on which the youth decided that there should be no authoritative roles and that all members should be considered equal in terms of role and responsibility. After several months of working together, however, the young people felt in desperate need of leadership and wanted to expand their organizational structure. They decided to create a number of leadership roles and hold elections to fill these new positions.

One young man was elected project director. At first, the young man was very unsure of himself; he had no role models in the program to imitate and no defined responsibilities. After struggling for a few days with his new role, he showed up in a suit and tie, holding a clipboard and an agenda. He had a completely formal management style with a list of tasks for the others in the group. The environment had been created in which he could begin to take risks and perform a "head taller" than who he had been earlier in the program. Simultaneously, the youth in the program began to see this young man *as* a leader—*as who he was becoming*.

Some aspects of this performance turned out to be very useful, but the group made it clear to him that he needed to "lighten up." Off came the suit and tie, but the clipboard and agenda remained—and so did the confidence and posture he gained from his new position in the group. With the ongoing support of the group, this young man became one of the most soft-spoken yet powerful leaders I have ever seen, completely transforming the way the group and the program operated. He was able to take criticism and feedback and gained the respect and admiration of all the young people in the program.

In youth participatory evaluations I often see that as roles change and develop, so do the programs—or is it that as the programs change and develop, so do the young people and their roles? Either way, through the activity of continually transforming their programs and communities and the authoritative roles within them, young people do indeed create powerful new roles and actions. In many cases, including the one in the sidebar, I have seen young people literally transform the nature of what it means to be in power.

DEVELOPMENT AND PLAY

Like performance, play has been understood as fundamental to human development. In fact, it could be said that performance is just one type of play. The importance of play is most frequently discussed in relation to early childhood development, but I would argue that play is important throughout the life cycle. Play allows us to break out of our traditionally cognitive and linear brain functions and supports radically new kinds of learning through movement, sound, poetry, song, "nonsense," and other creative thought processes.

Why is play important in evaluation? Play offers solutions for a number of challenges inherent in conducting evaluations. For many years evaluation has been understood as a practice conducted by "experts" or "scientists." Even as the field has moved toward more participatory and inclusive practices, staff members and youth are often intimidated by the prospect of being involved in evaluation. Playing with evaluation concepts and methods helps level the playing field so that staff and youth can begin to see evaluation as something that everyone can do.

A second challenge is that evaluations produce data and information that are often seen as irrelevant to both staff and youth. Program staff and participants often tell me that the evaluations of their programs have not at all represented their work or their values. By using play in evaluation, it is possible to invite staff and youth to participate in creating evaluation methods and instruments that more appropriately reflect their work, in both content and process. Organizations can develop methods that mirror the types of practices they have with youth. For example, youth theater programs might create ways of collecting data that are based in performance, youth organizing programs might build off of their community-based action research practices, and dance programs might develop physical methods for data collection. By framing evaluation as something that can be "played with" and reshaped, program staff and youth participants come to own the process. For evaluation to be truly participatory, it is important to relate to it as something that can and should be revised and built on.

The third challenge is that evaluation is generally an activity of "not knowing," of exploration. We live in a society in which knowing is extremely important. The role of "knower" has become central to our way of being in the world. People must know, or they will be seen as dumb or unsophisticated. Consequently, most people strive to be consummate "knowers" and have developed extremely powerful performances. These knowing performances, however, often prevent us from asking questions, from being curious, from experimenting, and perhaps even from developing. Play helps create an environment in which it is OK *not to know*.

I believe that my job as an evaluator is to help both youth participants and adult staff members become more curious and to develop the capacity to raise more questions about their practices. In the beginning of an evaluation project, much work must be done to support both youth and adults to become curious about their work. It is often difficult for staff and youth to create evaluation questions because they do not know how to ask questions, not being a practice they are familiar with. Some clients don't want to develop evaluation questions because they do not want me to know what they do *not* know about their organizations. Consequently, in the beginning of our work together, we do a lot of creative play that supports the activity of questioning and "not knowing."

Rather than facilitating knowing the right answer, creating playful environments allows people to move in and around the issues to learn in new and unique ways. This process helps groups think "outside the box" and encourages them to create their own unique forms of evaluation, not necessarily those that are born of traditional modes of logic.

The fourth challenge concerns the relationship between adults and youth. Play is important in YPE because it levels the playing field. When planning for a participatory evaluation with youth, I often send an agenda for my clients (most of whom are adults) to review. The agenda is generally packed full of play and performance activities, and my clients generally say something like "That will be so great for the young people; they will really enjoy that. What will the staff be doing?" When I tell them that I expect the group to work together on these activities, most adults are taken aback: "But I'm not a performer. Can't I just watch?" or "I don't know how to draw." They think the games will make them look ridiculous or, even worse, vulnerable in front of their colleagues and the young people. I explain that these types of playful activities facilitate a truly participatory environment, one that allows everyone to be involved and create together. I assure them that they will not have to do anything that will make them uncomfortable and encourage them to stay open to the possibility of participating. Inevitably, on the day of the workshop, the adults are right in there playing with the young people, often with equal enthusiasm and intensity. The opportunity to engage in play is very rare in our normal schedules, but when we are given permission to play, it is amazing how freeing it is to our minds, bodies, and souls. To let go of the usual societal controls is terrifying—we literally do not know what will happen next—but at the same time exhilarating—we come to new ways of thinking and understanding.

The last challenge is staying in the moment and actually listening and learning. Play allows participants to be absolutely "present." It demands that they stay focused in the moment and learn to work together with their "playmates." There are no theories to stand behind, no agendas to figure out, no external powers to be beholden to, only human beings in a room playing a game. Playful activity can be absolutely transformative. If you don't believe me, try it yourself!

TRANSFORMATION OF TOTALITIES AND DEVELOPMENT

Lev Vygotsky has gained popularity in the field of developmental psychology in recent decades. Many theorists and practitioners have come to understand the ZPD as an actual space (a zone) that can be measured in order to see the difference between the actual developmental level

IF THIS ORGANIZATION WERE A MOVIE

When I am working with a new program, I often use an icebreaker called "If This Organization Were a Movie." The first objective of this exercise is for the group to come up with a title for a movie about the organization. One youth group I worked with came up with the title "It's All About the Kids"; another came up with "School Invaders." Once the group has a title, I ask the participants to identify the movie's genre—science fiction, soap opera, and so forth. The group shouts out answers while I write them on a flip chart. Next, the group is asked to decide on the stars, costars, and supporting cast of the movie. After we sort out the various roles in the organization, I ask the group to decide which famous actors would play each of the characters and why. Everyone laughs and has a great time coming up with the most appropriate stars to play themselves and their colleagues.

I am always intrigued by this process. In many cases, groups work very collectively, shouting out possibilities for one another, making statements like "No, that isn't at all like you; you are like so-and-so." With one group, I remember an executive director who thought she should be played by Zena the Warrior Princess. Her staff thought she should be played by Geena Davis. They went back and forth on this issue for some time and finally agreed on Geena Davis. What I found fascinating was the degree to which the executive director allowed and encouraged staff feedback about her role and position in the organization, eventually becoming convinced that her views of herself weren't exactly the views of the staff and youth.

Once a group has figured out all aspects of the movie, I ask the participants if they would give me a one- or two-minute performance of the movie. (In all my years of working with youth, staff, funders, and executive directors, no one has ever denied my request to perform. In fact, people are thrilled because they have truly enjoyed the activity of playing.) Because they are already having a great time playing together, group members jump into the performance with ease and true excitement. During these one-minute performances, I have had program staff perform issues ranging from full-out staff fights to racial and gender issues to challenges they have working in schools to issues with their boards of directors. After a performance is finished, I generally ask the group to tell me which aspects of the performance were realistic and which were completely fictional.

This question generates honest conversations about the organization and its successes and challenges, both internally and externally.

I never directly ask a group to tell me about any of the challenges the organization faces, but by the end of the exercise I have a very clear picture of how the program operates and how the staff and youth communicate with each other. In these one-minute performances I come to understand so much more about the program than I would have learned by talking with the individuals involved. Staff and youth tell me that they too learn a lot about their own practices and relationships.

This exercise creates a safe environment in which people can play with the issues at hand—rather than tell me the "truth" about them. There is no moral judgment in play; participants are free to exaggerate some aspects of their work, which leads to very interesting discoveries by all. The performances are never really the "truth" but something more, a *creative imitation*. Performance can break out from under the weight of truth. Play is not about truth or logic; it is about participation, collaboration, creativity, and "not knowing."

and what is just beyond a young person's development. However, while learning and development are seen as social and cultural activities that occur between instructor and student, the instruction itself is often carefully manipulated and planned by adult teachers and facilitators, limiting the dialectical and participatory nature of the learning.

On the other hand, as I noted earlier, other theorists and practitioners believe that ZPDs are created through ongoing relational activity (Newman & Holzman, 1996). In this framework, it is not the job of the instructor to measure the ZPD and teach within it; it is the work of the group to create as many ZPDs as possible so that everyone can develop. In other words, the focus of the activity is not so much on the individual's development as it is on the group's development. As Lois Holzman explains, "Learning and development occur by the ongoing process of creating environments or groups for joint activity, in which you can perform past where you are at the moment" (2004, p. 5). Holzman pushes the boundaries of this notion of development as a social, cultural, and relational activity:

The unit that grows, that develops, that learns, is a social unit, not an individual unit. . . . We live our lives in groups, but we don't do it very well. We tend to think that groups are just collections of individuals. The unit that grows, that develops, that learns, is the social unit, not an individual unit. Groups grow [p. 5].

From this perspective social development is understood as "the joint activity of creating groups in order to learn, to grow, to give help, to get help, to create culture" (p. 5).

This understanding of development helps make the connection between individual, group, programmatic, and community development. Holzman argues that through the creation of environments, ZPDs come to exist. Through YPE projects, youth and adults create multiple ZPDs as they transform groups, programs, and often communities into environments that continue to support their growth.

Karl Marx's philosophy suggests that activity in which totalities are transformed is the very essence of human history. It is by participating in this type of activity (practical, critical, revolutionary activity) that we come to change the circumstances of our continued historical existence. As a Marxist psychologist, Vygotsky built on this notion of practical, critical, revolutionary activity to highlight its developmental nature, arguing that such activity is the source of both individual and social development.

The distinction between development as something that happens to you or is obtained versus something that is socially created is key in understanding the relationship between the various benefits attributed to YPE. The social creation theory demonstrates a relationship between individual and their environments. From this perspective development occurs through the activity of transforming totalities (organizations, programs, groups, societies), which helps us see how youth development might occur through youth evaluation and community research. After all, the primary objective for conducting YPE projects is usually not individual learning or skill development; rather, it is about creating environments with youth that support their development and growth—in other words, it is about transforming totalities.

Not many environments support people (particularly youth) to engage in this fundamentally human practical and critical activity of changing totalities. Instead, we have been taught to adapt to the environments in which we live. We are expected to act in our prescribed societal roles. Young people in particular live their lives in institutions that insist that they "behave" and perform the roles allotted them. As Shirley Brice Heath notes, there are few opportunities for young people to "act outside the constraints of the expected role of student or the structure of curricular and extra-curricular requirements" (2000, p. 39).

ZPDS AND CHANGING TOTALITIES

Once when I was directing a youth street theater group in Harlem, a fight broke out between two young men. This fight had been brewing for several weeks, both in the program and at school. All of the young people were from the same school and went to the same class, except one young man who was in a separate special education class. The other young people in the program had very little opportunity to interact with this young man during school, and their primary relationship was to tease and make fun of him during lunch and gym. What the young people "knew" for sure about this boy was that he was "different" from them.

In our theater program, the young people were forced to interact and work with the young man as an equal. None of the children, including the boy from special education, were at all sure that this was a good idea. Understandably, the young man was very angry with the others, often picking fights with them even when they weren't taunting him. The situation became very tense as the anger and hostility grew daily. My colleague and I had not yet found a way to fix the situation. No matter how much we talked about it with the group or tried to instill our morality on the participants, the tension grew.

On the day that the fight broke, this young man and another boy in the program were engaged in a full-blown fistfight on the floor of the community center before my colleague and I got to them. At first we began trying to pull them apart (not the most effective strategy for two women who are much smaller than the boys). Suddenly my colleague did something truly outside the box. While I was trying to separate the young men, she tackled me, screaming and cursing. I was confused. I couldn't get my bearings. What was happening? Then I realized she was "performing" what the boys were doing. I quickly moved into performance mode and jumped in, using their words: "I hate you, you are so stupid." F—— you!" my colleague yelled. "No, F—— you!" I shouted back. My

Adults' negative perceptions of youth as incapable, dangerous, and generally problematic continue to hold youth in their prescribed roles (James, 1997).

By involving young people in evaluation and community research, we are providing them with unique opportunities to engage in development

colleague and I were rolling around on the floor next to the two boys as all the young people laughed. The two boys who were fighting stopped and looked at us in bewilderment. "What are you doing?" one of them asked. "We're performing you," we answered. They stared at us blankly and then one of boys said, "That isn't what I did. I said, "Why are you acting stupid and then I pushed him." "OK," I answered, "like this?" and I performed the actions as he directed me. My colleague and I let the boys direct us until we got the "fight scene" just right. The activity transformed immediately from two boys fighting to two boys working together to direct my colleague and me in the "fight scene."

Next, something even more surprising happened. Other young people from the group began to tell us their roles in the "fight scene." One young girl said, "My role was as the instigator. I've been doing everything I could to make them fight all morning." "Great," I said, "that's a terrific role to add to our play." We asked the group to tell us what other roles existed in the "fight scene." In other words, what other material did we have to work with?

Rather than relating to the fight as bad behavior, we related to it as material from which to create a performance, highlighting that these were all just roles that we could play or one possible choice of character. Each young person told us how he or she had contributed to the "fight scene." We started the play over from the beginning, with all of the different performers involved. What they performed with us was a very complex social scene that had started earlier in the day. It was a very interesting performance, fraught with issues of exclusion, violence, hostility, and nastiness. At the end of the performance my colleague and I clapped and said, "Wow, what a terrifically offensive performance, truly ugly. What do you all think of it?" The young people agreed with us—it wasn't their best performance. This was not at all a moral statement about the children; it was about the play itself.

(both their own and society's). As young people perform in these roles, they simultaneously transform them and come to see themselves as participants in the creation of (perhaps new) societal roles and begin to understand their significance in history and their power as agents of change. Thus they are reconnected with the process of their own historical development.

To the extent that empowerment and youth development "interventions" continue to be understood as top-down techniques to get people involved in *democracy* (as created and defined by politicians) and to acquire *critical understanding, learning, and skills* (as defined by outside academics and experts) in order to gain *power* (which is situated in a capitalistic society of "haves" and "have-nots"), we have missed the fundamentally relational, practical, and critical nature of human beings as defined by Marx. Development, and indeed empowerment, lies in the continuous activity of collectively creating something new, something not defined in a priori fashion using a priori methods.

2

DESIGNING AND CONDUCTING YOUTH PARTICIPATORY EVALUATION PROJECTS

Practitioners who are reading this book might be wondering, "YPE sounds great in theory, but just how do we put it into practice?" In Part Two, I would like to share with you some of the practices my colleagues and I have experimented with over the years. These chapters outline the key activities necessary to conduct a YPE process and highlight a myriad of playful, performatory activities that support the creation of developmental environments. The purpose is not so much to explain how to conduct a full evaluation—many books have already been written on this subject—but to provide you with playful developmental activities that can be used with a YPE team.

CHAPTER

STARTING YOUR OWN YPE PROJECT

When you have finished reading this chapter, you will know more about the following:

- How to select youth for participation in a YPE project

- The optimal number of youth to work with in a YPE project

- Whether or not to compensate youth for their participation in YPE projects

- How old a person needs to be to participate in a YPE project

- The value of engaging youth of different ages and capacities in YPE projects

- Who should facilitate the YPE process

- The challenges of conducting a YPE project in a program that is not participatory

- How to engage and prepare additional stakeholders in the YPE project

Beginning a YPE project brings up many questions, the most common ones including these:

Do youth really want to participate in evaluation?

Which youth should participate?

How many youth should be involved?

Should youth be compensated for their participation?

How old does someone have to be to participate?

What is the value of engaging youth of different ages and capacities?

Can youth really conduct effective and useful evaluations that we can trust?

Who should facilitate the YPE process?

What happens when a YPE project is conducted in a program that is not participatory?

How do we engage and prepare additional stakeholders in the process, particularly those in positions of power?

I don't have definitive answers to every question, but I will share my thoughts and experiences from the past decade of working with YPE projects, both in the United States and around the world. I am sure you will come up with many more questions, answers, and examples as you embark on your own YPE projects.

DO YOUTH REALLY WANT TO PARTICIPATE IN EVALUATION?

People often ask me, "Kim, how do you get young people to conduct evaluations? It seems like it would be so boring for them." This question is most often asked by adults. I've never had a young person ask it.

We are born evaluators. It is what we do. In fact, I find it much harder to stop people from evaluating than to engage them in the process. During my training sessions, people are continuously evaluating the temperature, the food, my attire, their peers, and so many other things. They simply don't think of it as evaluation. When working with youth, I generally start from where they are—asking them to define and uncover the ways that they already use evaluation in their everyday lives.

Performance and play techniques further help youth (and adults) feel that they can engage in and play with evaluation. Both young people and adults come to see that it really isn't so difficult. Through play, evaluation becomes demystified and far less dry. In my experience, youth really enjoy working on YPE projects.

WHICH YOUTH SHOULD PARTICIPATE?

Whether the YPE positions are paid or volunteer, the selection of young people can be difficult and sometimes dicey. The easiest way to identify possible participants is to explain the project to all the young people in the program and ask for volunteers, accepting anyone who steps forward. Often, however, for a variety of programmatic and funding reasons, I am not able to engage all the young people who are interested in participating in a project. Many of my colleagues have had similar experiences. In these instances we engage in a selection process. Whatever process we use, we make certain that it is transparent and that all youth have an equal chance to participate, even if they ultimately opt out. One very important point: do not handpick a team, as this creates a very heated situation among the young people—particularly when certain privileges are given to the YPE team members, such as stipends, salary, or other incentives. One strategy I have seen work well incorporates the following steps:

1. At a large group meeting, explain the YPE project to all youth. Tell them the number of hours you think the project will take per week, what it will entail, which skills they might learn, and, if applicable, the amount of money the job is paying. Let everyone in the program know that you will be interviewing young people for the team.

2. Ask the group to help you develop criteria from which to select the team. For example, you might ask the group to brainstorm the following questions:

- What qualities do you think a youth team member might need?

- What types of skills might team members need?

- What types of interests might they have?

- To ensure that the program is evaluated from multiple perspectives, we need to make sure that people with different viewpoints are included on the team. Should we make sure to include particular perspectives (culture, politics, gender, educational background or experiences)? If so, which ones?

3. Once the full set of criteria have been developed, the application and interview process can begin. You might develop a selection committee made up of youth and adults who will review applications and interview the young people. Make certain to select young people who are excited about participating and fully understand the project and its commitments. Also, to the extent possible, create a YPE team of young people who are representative of all youth in the program in terms of age, gender, ethnicity, and ability. In this way the YPE team can explore all the issues in a given program more comprehensively.

HOW MANY YOUTH SHOULD BE INVOLVED?

Over the years, I have seen programs involve as few as three and as many as forty young people on the evaluation team, depending on the scope of the work to be done and the level of enthusiasm of youth in the program. Another factor is the amount of time and energy a program can spend on the YPE project.

SHOULD YOUTH BE COMPENSATED FOR THEIR PARTICIPATION?

Yeah, we think that being paid well is really important. It's like "Look, OK I can sell dope for two hours and I'll get like $300, like two blocks away, or I'll go make $200 per day with some businessmen who work at a corporate bank. So, I mean, even while this salary doesn't compete with that, it is still a good job. What it told me was that somebody really cares about my experiences and somebody really thinks I'm smart and somebody really thinks that I should be paid well and I'm only seventeen.

Woman, age 17, participating in a project in California
focused on young women in the sex trade

Young people have told me repeatedly that the compensation for their involvement in the evaluation was very important to them. The fact that they were paid well made them feel valued and part of the team; the work became very real to them and not merely an academic exercise like those in school. Many young people have used these experiences on their résumés and were able to get work using their new skill set. Young people clearly see they are providing valuable services to a program and feel that they should be compensated for their efforts. In this way, they come to see the work more like a job, a view that increases their commitment to the process.

HOW OLD DOES SOMEONE HAVE TO BE TO PARTICIPATE?

At some point, everyone ends up asking me this question. I think the urgency for an answer stems from the prevalent belief in Piaget's theory of development, which outlines multiple stages of development that are often tied to age. In this approach, if development occurs at a specific age, we are then able to use age-appropriate materials to teach a young person. Although numerous alternative views emphasize the social, cultural, and individual differences that influence both learning and development, most people still understand development as something that needs to occur before learning can happen.

In contrast, as discussed earlier in this book, Lev Vygotsky made a unique contribution to the field of child development that points to a different type of relationship between learning and development, one in which learning leads development instead of the other way around. Vygotsky (1978) observes, "Any learning worthy of the name leads development." Indeed, instruction "wakens a whole series of functions that are in a stage of maturation lying in the zone of proximal development" (p. 212). If we think about development from this perspective, it is necessary to create instruction that is in advance of a child's actual development. Holzman and Newman go further, arguing that it is not enough to develop specific types of instruction that are in advance of a child's development; rather, the task is to continuously create environments that are rich in ZPDs, so that everyone can learn. It is through the continuous, collaborative activity of creating the environment that people come to grow and develop (Holzman, 1997; Newman & Holzman, 1993).

From this standpoint, I argue that anyone of any age can be involved in YPE projects. The objective is to create a group that is inclusive of all participants and that can support the group's growth. In my experience, the age of the young person is irrelevant—the task needs to be very creative, allowing the skills (and lack of skills) to guide the process. The trick is to build with what you have, supporting the young people to create and use methods that are meaningful to the group.

My friend and colleague Roger Hart has written extensively on the subject of how to include young children as citizens who monitor and evaluate their community's development and environmental care. His book *Children's Participation* (1997) provides a myriad of methods and strategies for engaging very young children in research and evaluation.

WHAT IS THE VALUE OF ENGAGING YOUTH OF DIFFERENT AGES AND CAPACITIES?

Often YPE teams are made up of youth of similar ages, but I enjoy working with young people of different ages and capacities in a given program. Such diversity encourages the YPE team members to grapple with the multiple perspectives, views, and capacities of everyone in the program. Also, age diversity offers even more opportunities to collectively create and build with one another, affording an environment rich with ZPDs.

YPE teams consisting of multiple ages and capacities bring a wide array of assets, understandings, and experiences to the table. To function well, these groups have to work hard to create environments in which everyone can learn and develop together. In my experience, this activity provides fertile ground for the continuous creation of ZPDs and ongoing human development.

CAN YOUNG PEOPLE REALLY CONDUCT EFFECTIVE AND USEFUL EVALUATIONS THAT WE CAN TRUST?

I think the real question being asked is, Can young people do what "trained professional evaluators" do? The answer? Of course not. These two practices are not the same. Evaluators are trained for many years in social science methods and understand a myriad of theories and practices. In fact, that is the value of having the support of a trained evaluation coach. As a professional evaluator, I offer a very specific understanding of a field that I have had the time and privilege to study. My asset, if you will, is that I bring my evaluation knowledge to the table and support young people to conduct projects that are truly meaningful to them. On the other hand, the young people know the content of the program, they understand how it works, and they understand how youth think, behave, and talk to one another. I share my knowledge with them, and they share theirs with me, and on a great day we both end up with very different understandings of both youth and evaluation.

Is their work "statistically significant"? No, not often. But it is rigorous and brings together multiple points of view, at multiple times, using multiple methods. I believe that the YPE evaluation strategies, methods, and findings are often more important, more effective, and certainly more useful to programs than mine would be if I were to work as an outside evaluation consultant.

WHO SHOULD FACILITATE THE YPE PROCESS?

The YPE process occurs in a number of ways: a program staff member works with an evaluation consultant, a group of staff members and a team of youth work with an evaluation consultant, or a youth leader works with an evaluation consultant or program director. The titles of the participants are not so important, but there should be at least one person on the team who has a good understanding of the program and its participants and at least one person who understands and knows how to facilitate an evaluation process.

In selecting the team of facilitators, there are several factors to consider. First, in working with an outside evaluator, it is important to make sure that he or she understands youth development practices—not just from a theoretical point of view but from practical hands-on experiences. Preferably this person would have values and practices that mirror those within the program or organization. Second, the evaluator should be able to translate social science language and practices into something that is recognizable to youth. Third, the evaluator should be willing to listen attentively to the youth and employ democratic participatory strategies—and not bring a personal research agenda to the table that cannot be influenced and shaped by the young people. Fourth, it is important to determine if the person is truly interested in the development of the youth, the program, and himself or herself.

WHAT HAPPENS WHEN A YPE PROJECT IS CONDUCTED IN A PROGRAM THAT IS NOT PARTICIPATORY?

In 1998 I was studying a youth participatory evaluation process in a Canadian inner-city shelter. An adult evaluation consultant and several young people in the program were conducting a study of the shelter and its impacts on the community. The process was both labor-intensive and extremely rewarding and participatory. The adult evaluation coach truly valued the views and input of the young people and treated them as important contributors to all aspects of the evaluation process.

This type of inclusion and participation was extremely rare in the context of the shelter, and not surprisingly, it affected the young people in profound ways. They were honored to be part of program decision making, and they had the opportunity to develop a new kind of relationship with an adult. The young people had much to say about this new and unique type of relationship. Not only did they enjoy their newfound voices in the context of the YPE project, but they began to feel more empowered in the community.

However, at the end of the evaluation effort, the key adult decision makers in the shelter and in the community were unwilling to take the YPE team's findings and recommendations seriously. In fact, the adults did not even bother to tell the young people why their recommendations were not considered or implemented.

By the end of the YPE project, the youth, who previously had very positive feelings about their participation, felt that their work didn't matter because it had no real impact. They were unable to make the kinds of changes they wanted to see in the program and became even more dissatisfied. The project reinforced the youth's feelings that their voices did not matter in the world.

This example highlights the need to guarantee young people an opportunity to express themselves once the data are collected and analyzed. To the extent possible, adult facilitators and key youth leaders should begin conversations with the key adult decision makers from the very start of the evaluation project. This provides a concrete understanding of just how open the key adult decision makers will be to the youth's voices and recommendations. In situations where adult decision makers cannot change certain aspects of the project or program due to funding or other restraints, it is important that youth evaluators understand which aspects of the program they can influence and focus their attention on them. Whatever the situation, it is better to understand the dynamics before embarking on a YPE project.

At the beginning of a project numerous conversations should be held with key adult stakeholders. In most cases, adult staff members know very little about program evaluation and are often intimidated by it. I recommend being as clear as possible about why youth input is valuable to the program.

Optimally, a YPE project will be conducted in a program that is open to change and eager to engage youth in decision making. I have been involved in numerous YPE processes that have supported youth views both in the programs and in the organizations. This type of evaluation process helps programs develop sustainable structures for engaging young people in long-term programmatic decision making. This is the best scenario and requires that adults be extremely open to change. Youth in Focus, in the book *Youth REP Step by Step: An Introduction to Youth-Led Research and Evaluation* (2002), has done a great job of identifying some of the key organizational qualities that need to be in place to support youth participation in evaluation.

Organizational Culture

■ The insights, experiences, and capacities of youth are valued and respected.

■ There is a commitment to youth and community development processes that build on strengths while recognizing and addressing challenges.

■ Strong relationships and communication between staff and youth and between staff and community are highly valued.

■ Diversity (ethnic, cultural, linguistic, and so on) is considered an asset.

■ Youth are supported as active leaders and participants in research, evaluation, and planning processes.

Organizational Structure

■ Decision-making processes include youth and other community constituents.

■ Channels of communication are accessible to and actively used by youth and other community constituents.

■ Strong communication between organization staff and leadership is valued.

■ Organizational stability includes aspects such as solid finances and low staff turnover.

- Staff-youth ratios allow for personalized, supportive facilitation for the youth team.

- Existing systems facilitate needs assessment and evaluation or a strong intent to establish such systems.

- Expectations of staff and youth-community constituents are high and fair.

- Capacity to allocate or raise required funds supports youth REP (research, evaluation and planning) and related activities.

Of course, these are optimal conditions! Evaluators are not always privileged to work in such programs. Hopefully, the answers to some of the remaining questions will provide strategies to negotiate more challenging circumstances.

HOW DO WE ENGAGE AND PREPARE ADDITIONAL STAKEHOLDERS IN THE PROCESS, PARTICULARLY THOSE IN POSITIONS OF POWER?

The strongest YPE projects occur when all stakeholders are engaged in the process (particularly those holding the most power in the organization—typically adults). The most successful YPE projects I have been involved with trained both adults and youth in the program. Depending on the circumstances, this training can either be conducted in a parallel manner (with youth and adults in separate sessions), or it can be interconnected (with youth and adults learning about evaluation together). Or a combination of both approaches can be used, with some sessions conducted with all members of the team and some with specific groupings. Having both youth and adults build their evaluations is important for four reasons. First, adults often have their own fears about evaluation, and they too need to learn more so they are able to support the YPE team in their efforts. Second, when adults are engaged, they begin to value the views of the young people in the program and are more likely to hear and respond to their YPE findings and recommendations. Third, adults in the program have valuable perspectives to contribute to the evaluation project. Fourth, adults and youth tend to develop very different types of relationships with one another when they are creating knowledge together.

CHAPTER

DEVELOPING THE ENSEMBLE YPE TEAM

When you have finished reading this chapter, you will know more about the following:

- How to build an ensemble in which youth and adults can productively create together

- How to use performance terminology to set the stage for working as an ensemble

- How to move from the role of adult facilitator to performance director

- How to build with all that is in the room (both what is perceived to be positive and what is perceived to be negative)

- How to learn more about what young people, think, feel, and know about evaluation

- How to help the YPE team members really listen to one another

- How to help youth learn more about evaluation terminology

- How to create rules with the YPE team

- How to identify roles for the YPE team

- How to monitor the YPE team

The evaluation consultant taught us that the only thing that separates academics from other people is language, and once you can get past language and learn the language, there is no difference besides maybe a piece of paper and some years of school.

Shaniqua, age 18

Shaniqua said this to me while I was interviewing her for my dissertation, and it made sense. I did not know the language of evaluation yet, nor did I have a piece of paper stating that I was a bona fide evaluator, but I did have a strong belief that we are all born evaluators. It is part of how we operate and negotiate the world. We move through our days assessing our likes and dislikes, comparing our past experiences with our present. The only difference between professional evaluators and everyone else is that the professionals know how to gather information systematically using scientific methods and how to frame their work in the language of the field. Although these are significant skills, they can be learned by most people. The difficulty is creating an environment in which people can perform as evaluators.

The performances of evaluation and research have typically been assigned to well-educated academicians. Typically, the average person does not believe he or she has the skills and the smarts to do this type of work. This is certainly the case with young people. Learning institutions and the adults who work in them often reinforce this belief by letting youth know that they are consumers of knowledge, not creators of it.

Work is needed to change these power dynamics and create environments in which all participants can become knowledge creators. In this chapter, I will share a range of creative activities that can be used to build an ensemble in which youth and adults can productively create together.

GETTING STARTED

From the very first moment of a YPE project, it is important to build a creative, performatory environment. I find it useful to use theater language, such as "ensemble," "performance," "creativity," "play," and "roles." This vocabulary lets the YPE team know that the creative activity of building the ensemble is just as important as the product or data that we generate. To create this type of creative space, the ensemble must come to understand that there are no wrong answers and that everyone will be viewed as having something important to add to the project. The work of the group is to figure out creatively how to use and build on everything the group has to offer. The objective is to create an environment in which the entire YPE team (including the adults) feel comfortable performing beyond themselves—as who they are becoming. As I have mentioned previously, you can create a YPE team with only youth, with youth and adults working separately, or with youth and adults working collectively. The choice is yours. However, throughout the following activities I will most frequently talk about the YPE team as a youth-only grouping. Remember to make the work playful, creative, and nonjudgmental.

So let's get started!

MOVING FROM ADULT FACILITATOR TO PERFORMANCE DIRECTOR

Conducting a YPE project might be one of the most challenging activities you will ever do, particularly if you are interested in the developmental model I am describing in this book. However, I guarantee that it will also be one of the most rewarding experiences of your life. I have grown and developed beyond my wildest dreams due to my work with both youth and adults who are committed to creating truly inclusive and developmental environments.

Don't let your own fear and inexperience stop you from moving forward—use it, build with it. The most important tip I can offer is this: build with everything you can find—the good, the bad, and especially the ugly. Most of us are not good at building with things we dislike. Instead, we get rid of them or try to modify them; we create rules about them, work around them, ignore them. We will do anything to avoid embracing the ugly and turning it to our advantage.

This is where performance comes in. When we are in the theater, we have no trouble embracing all of the "material" available to us. In fact, it is a requirement. This is how plays are created; performers and directors use the script, the emotions of the character, the emotions of the actor, the vision of the directors, the words and emotions of the playwright, and so forth. As a YPE facilitator, one of your most important performances is to become an expert at building with what the young people are giving you.

IMPROVISATION: BUILDING WITH WHAT YOU HAVE

A number of years ago I had the opportunity to work in a Vygotskian laboratory school in New York City. The school was made up of a small number of young people aged five to fifteen. They were a diverse bunch, representing a wide range of ethnicities, sociocultural backgrounds, and IQs. Everyone in the school was responsible for building the learning environment. Children often found instruction outside of school and were encouraged to use the city as part of their development. One day the students took a trip to visit a musician who was going to teach them to play the guitar. The students had collectively decided that one young man would stay at the school because he was having a difficult time and did not want to participate and that I would stay with him. As he and I watched out the window as the others left, he suddenly got very upset. He found a handful of marbles and began throwing them at the windows. He was throwing pretty hard, and I was terrified he was going to break one of the windows. At first I got reactive and tried everything I knew to make him stop. Then it occurred to me to "perform" with what he

The role I most often draw on is that of director, the person leading the play. When you start "playing around" with this role, take time to step back from the play now and then and look at what you are creating. Look with your "director eyes," and you will find yourself seeing differently. As you come to see the team's work as a theatrical ensemble, you will be able to give stage notes and help redirect the play.

Most theater directors say they work with actors for months to perfect their parts and make a play work. Directors try every possible combination of emotions, behaviors, costumes, props, and music. In theater, cast members are comfortable with the notion of rehearsal: you keep trying new things until something clicks. This is the perspective I recommend while facilitating a YPE project.

The activities in the rest of the book have been used successfully with many different groups, and I hope you will find them useful in your own work. Of course, I have facilitated my share of exercises that bombed, but I've learned from them too. So have fun trying out these activities, and be sure to experiment and modify details to fit your team. And if an exercise doesn't work, create something new!

was giving me. I looked around the room, trying to figure out what I could build with—what props were available. He continued throwing marbles, with increasing velocity. There were marbles all over the floor. I eyed a piece of string—and then I had it. I quickly made a circle with the string and gathered up the marbles, placing them inside the circle. I began shooting them, one by one, out of the circle. I played quietly by myself for several minutes before I caught his attention. He looked at me after a bit and asked, "What are you doing?" "Playing marbles," I answered. He was curious. "How do you play?" I showed him the moves, and he and I played together quietly, talking about the different angles that are necessary for effective marble shooting. We learned a lot about one another during this activity, but mostly we learned how to play and perform together.

In this situation, I stopped reacting to his marble-throwing performance and began figuring out how to create another, less dangerous performance. I stopped being judgmental about his behavior and started trying to build with what he was giving me. He was giving me marbles, so I used marbles to create a new play.

DISCOVERING ALL THAT THE YPE TEAM MEMBERS HAVE TO OFFER

Anyone who has conducted or participated in an evaluation project (participatory or otherwise) knows that it elicits a wide range of emotions. Rather than deny these feelings, build with them. Even if they are not overtly expressed, they will still be in the room and in the work.

I cannot stress enough that prior to beginning any evaluation process, the values, perspectives, and views of the participants must be unpacked and understood so that the YPE team can begin to play with these concepts and think about whether and how they relate to the work the team is about to undertake.

Next I describe three activities that I use to get groups talking about past experiences with evaluation: the Human Survey, Reflection on a Word, and Defining YPE. You can use one, two, or all three, depending on the needs of your particular team.

EVALUATION IS A SCARY SUBJECT During one stakeholder meeting with a group of staff members, we conducted an activity to determine what the experiences and views of the staff were regarding evaluation. It became apparent that staff members believed that the goal of the stakeholder meeting was to evaluate their job perform-ance. Although the executive director had tried to be very clear about the participatory *evaluation* process and the staff's role in it, the staff heard the word *evaluation* and panicked. The word called up so many negative images that they quickly went into defense mode and did not want to par-ticipate. This is a fairly common reaction. Evaluation has so many negative connotations that almost everyone has an evaluation horror story to tell.

Activity: The Human Survey

Objectives

- To break the ice and get the YPE team moving around

- To gain an understanding of the YPE team's beliefs, feelings, and experiences regarding evaluation

- To highlight and validate the YPE team members' current knowl-edge of evaluation and let them know they have something to offer

- To dispel some myths about evaluation

Steps

1. Start by telling the YPE team that you would like to understand more about each member's thoughts and feelings about evaluation. To accomplish this goal, you are going to conduct a Human Survey.

2. Create an imaginary straight line in the room; for example, pick a chair at one end and a door at the other. Ask the participants to stand at one end of the line (the chair, for example) if they "love evaluation," at the other end of the line (the door) if they "hate eval-uation," or anywhere in between the chair and the door to indicate their feelings.

3. Once they have made a decision about where to stand on this imaginary line, ask the participants why they chose to stand where

they are. Encourage different people to explain why they "hate evaluation," why they think it is "OK," and why they "love it." Let individuals share their stories with the group. Be sure to validate their experiences and assure them that you understand some of the difficulties with evaluation work. On your flipchart, note how many participants "hate" evaluation, how many think it is "OK," and how many "love it." Also note the rationales for their responses.

4. Next, have participants line up on the same imaginary line to reflect the extent of their experience with evaluation. Ask them to stand at one end of the imaginary line if they have "a lot of experience" and at the other if they have "no experience" with evaluation. Again, they can place themselves anywhere along the continuum to reflect their experience.

5. Once they have placed themselves along the imaginary line, ask a few participants to explain why they are standing where they are. Encourage YPE team members to say why they feel they have "little to no experience," "some experience," or "a lot of experience" with evaluation. On the flipchart, note how many participants have "no experience," how many have "some experience," and how many have "a lot of experience."

Note: During this exercise, young people will share their views and feelings about evaluation. Often they will provide examples of how they have been evaluated. The following questions are useful in guiding such a YPE team discussion:

Who typically does an evaluation? Why these people?

Why are evaluations conducted?

Is evaluation important? Why or why not?

Can anyone conduct an evaluation? Why or why not?

By understanding the YPE team members' views and feelings regarding evaluation, you can talk to them about participatory program evaluation and how it is similar to or different from other types of evaluations. As the facilitator, you might want to share your feelings about evaluation and describe the type of evaluation you are hoping to conduct with the YPE team.

Point out that the YPE team has just conducted its first survey and that the survey captured both qualitative and quantitative information.

For example, you were able to count the number of youth who "loved evaluation" and the number who "hated evaluation" and all of those in between. That constitutes quantitative data. You were also able to capture "qualitative" data about why they chose to stand where they did along the imaginary line.

Activity: Reflection on a Word

Objectives

- To elicit the young people's views and feelings about evaluation

- To deepen (either independently or in concert with the Human Survey) the conversation about evaluation and its various meanings

Steps

1. Begin this exercise by asking the participants to shout out the first thing they think of when you ask each of the following questions. Tell them not to think about their answers too much since there are no wrong answers. As they shout out answers, write them down on the flipchart.

2. Ask the following question: What is the first thing you think of when I say the word *evaluation?*

3. Once they have exhausted their responses, review and summarize what they have said. For example, "It seems like a lot of you think about being judged when you think of evaluation" or "It seems that very few of you think about improvement when you think of evaluation."

4. Create a discussion by asking some of the following questions: How did you come to this understanding of evaluation? Do you think there could be another use for evaluation? What might that be?

Note: You might want to go over the following points:

- The term *evaluation* has been used in many different ways in recent years, and the YPE team members have captured many of these definitions in their responses.

- There are many different types of evaluation: program evaluation, staff evaluation, psychological evaluation, and so forth. Sometimes the words used in evaluation can be very confusing because the field is new and often people use the same words to mean different things (such as *evaluation, assessment,* and *questionnaire*).

5. Ask the YPE team the following question: What is the first thing you think of when I say *participation*?

6. Once they have exhausted their responses, review and summarize what they have said. For example, "It seems like a lot of you think participation is about 'collaboration and teamwork,' and most of you think that it is different from evaluation."

7. Generate conversation by asking some of the following questions: How did you come to this understanding of participation? Have you ever been part of a participatory project or process? If so, what was that like? If not, how might you imagine it to be?

8. Ask this question: What is the first thing you think of when I say *participatory evaluation*?

9. Once they have exhausted their responses, review and summarize what they have said. For example, "It seems like a lot of you think participatory evaluation is about 'working together to evaluate something.' Some of you think it is similar to evaluation, and others think it is very different from evaluation."

10. Generate discussion by asking some of the following questions: How did you come to this understanding of participatory evaluation? What do you think makes participatory evaluation different from regular evaluation (as described in the very first question I asked)? In what ways is participatory evaluation the same as other types of evaluation?

Activity: Defining YPE

Objectives

- To support an in-depth understanding of YPE

- To give young people the opportunity to create their own definition for evaluation and the values they would like to uphold during their YPE process

- To increase the likelihood that youth will believe they can conduct a YPE project

Steps

1. Once the YPE team has finished with the Reflection on a Word activity, team members can use the words they have brainstormed to create their own definition of youth participatory evaluation and the principles they want to work by. Have the YPE team split into two groups. One can work on defining evaluation, and the other can develop the working principles.

2. Once the group members have completed their work, have them share what they have produced with one another and begin to discuss the various values and principals involved in YPE.

3. Next, you might want to supply the YPE team with the definitions professional evaluators have come up with so that they can compare and contrast their definitions with those from the field. In my experience, young people come very close to definitions used by Michael Quinn Patton (utilization-focused evaluation) and by David Fetterman (empowerment evaluation):

    Program evaluation is the systematic collection of information about the activities, characteristics, and outcomes of programs to make judgments about the program, improve program effectiveness, and/ or inform decisions about future programming. Utilization-focused program evaluation (as opposed to program evaluation in general) is evaluation done for and with specific, intended primary users for specific, intended uses [Patton, 1997, p. 23].

    Empowerment evaluation is the use of evaluation concepts, techniques, and findings to foster improvement and self-determination. It employs both qualitative and quantitative methodologies. Although it can be applied to individuals, organizations, communities, and societies or cultures, the focus is on programs. It is attentive to empowering processes and outcomes [Fetterman, Kaftarian, & Wandersman, 1996, p. 4].

Note: The purpose of sharing these definitions is not to provide youth with the "right answer" but to illustrate how much they already know about the subject and how others have defined the term.

4. Once participants have finalized their definitions, write them on the flipchart and have them in the room whenever the YPE team meets.

A NEW LANGUAGE FOR EVALUATION

While working with a small program located on an Indian reservation, the young people informed me that they could not relate to or understand my language. None of the words I was using made sense to them. Not only were my words too academic, but the evaluation terms themselves had no cultural basis in their community. Their heritage was based on a history and philosophy of weaving and "pulling" (a type of boat rowing particular to their culture). Their understanding of the world is based on the relational unities inherent in collective weaving and "pulling" rather than on the linearity, cause and effect, and particulars more common in Western culture. These differences made it difficult for me to use terms and concepts such as "strategic planning," "logic model," "theory of change," "outcomes," and "indicators."

After the young people identified these differences in beliefs and practices, they developed weaving and rowing analogies and terms for evaluation that more accurately reflected their experiences and understanding of their world and practice. In the end, they developed an evaluation process that allowed them to talk about "pulling together" and "weaving their stories."

PERFORMING THE ENSEMBLE

Once the YPE team members have explored their beliefs and views of participatory evaluation and have created working definitions and principles, they can begin creating the ensemble. In this section, I share three different activities: the "Yes, And ..." game is a theater exercise often used to teach improvisation skills. In the My Gift to the Group activity, young people create a visual representation of a particular asset or "gift" they are bringing to the YPE team. The third activity, Performing Me, requires the young people to create a one-minute performance about their lives. These performances are then used to develop a collective performance about the YPE team. These games can be used separately or together at any time during the YPE project.

Activity: The "Yes, And . . ." Game

Objectives

■ To build the ensemble

■ To explore a new way of listening and building together

■ To help the YPE team stay in the moment

■ To help the YPE team learn how to "not know"

Steps

1. Tell the YPE team about the activity, explaining that they will be creating a collective story, with each of the team members using only one sentence at a time. They will have to keep building the story based on the sentence that precedes theirs. In other words, they can't think of what they want to say prior to hearing what the person before them adds to the story. After each person says his or her sentence, the following person must say "yes, and . . ."—and then add a sentence. The *yes* marks acceptance, and the *and* marks a gift to the next person.

    Note: This exercise is commonly used in improvisation because it teaches performers to "stay in the moment" and listen closely to their partners. Too often in meetings and other group activities, we are already thinking of what we want to say while others are talking—we are not listening. Or we are thinking "no, but . . ." and are not listening. This exercise provides a new way of building a conversation that is less competitive and more performatory, with team members building something together.

    While creating the collective story, ask the YPE team members to listen attentively to what is said by the person preceding them in the circle so that they can build on that person's gift and continue to create the story. Stop the story if you hear anyone in the group say "no, but . . ." or break the storyline by failing to accept the offer of the previous player or to give a gift to the next player.

2. Begin by asking the members of the YPE team to come up with a title for their story. You may want to select a title that has something to do with evaluation or the YPE team, as it might provide

interesting information about the team members' thoughts and feelings regarding the work they are preparing to do.

3. Once the YPE team has selected a title, select one person to start the story. Remind everyone that each person can add only one sentence. Proceed around the room. After a person adds a sentence, the next person must accept the offer by answering with "yes, and . . ." and then adding a sentence. Go around the room two or three times or until the story comes to a logical end. At that point, say, "The end," and applaud the performance.

4. After the story is completed, ask the YPE team members to talk about their experience of the exercise. You might want to ask the following questions:

> Did you listen to one another differently?

> Did you hear any break in the flow of the story? If so, where? Why did you feel it was a break?

> Were you surprised by what you said or what the YPE team created?

> How was this conversation similar to or different from every-day conversations?

Note: Talk to the YPE team about the importance of having these types of conversations in which they really listen to one another and build the conversation rather than compete in it. You can expect some fascinating dialogue! Often participants say that they listened differently during this exercise or that they were more conscious of building with one another than in a normal conversation. Stress the importance of this type of listening and conversation building in creative environments.

Another point that might be discussed is how much easier it is to have a conversation when there is no "right" and "wrong," when there are no "truths," and when the speakers can make things up. Talk to the YPE team about the possibility of experimenting with this in real-life conversations, interviews, meetings, and focus groups; in other words, encourage team members not to stay so tightly tied to their "truth" but instead learn to build with what other people are giving them in conversations. This type of listening and building work facilitates effective practices in evaluation work.

REALLY LISTENING TO ONE ANOTHER

I once worked with the board of directors from a small family foundation that was very committed to doing quality work with young people, and the directors spent much of their time debating the best strategies for implementing their various agendas. This was a particularly tough environment because they were all family members and represented three different generations. Members of each generation had a different set of beliefs and values that guided their work. At some point I asked the group to play the "Yes, And . . ." game with me. We came up with a title, and the directors created a story together. Their story, like those of most

---

Activity: My Gift to the Group

Objectives

- To build the ensemble

- To help the young people articulate their assets and gifts to the YPE team

- To allow the YPE team members to recognize the skills and capacities they are working with so they can build with them later

Note: This ensemble-building activity requires that YPE team members create visual representations of what they intend to offer the group during the YPE process. Many different art materials can be used to create these visual representations, but I find that modeling clay has a special advantage: it allows team members to mold their individual sculptures and then join them together into a group sculpture. Often YPE teams like to save their sculptures and refer to them as they work together.

Steps

1. Explain the exercise to the YPE team. Let the participants know that you would like them to create a visual representation of the assets or skills (or both) that they have and would like to contribute to the group.

2. Have the team members work with the modeling clay until they feel confident with their creations. This should take fifteen to twenty minutes.

groups who play this game, was abstract and funny. The board members quickly realized that they were having great difficultly listening to one another. One of the elder family members confessed that as the story moved around the room, she felt she always had a better sentence than the person before her. By the time the story got to her, she began to realize that her performance as "knower" was prohibiting her from building with the group, from really listening to what the others had to offer. This little game was absolutely transformative for this foundation and began to change the way the directors communicated with one another at board meetings.

3. Once all of the young people have finished, ask them to explain their figures and why they represent their most prized gifts to the group.

4. When all of the YPE team members have discussed their sculptures, have them work together to create one sculpture that represents their efforts as a group, assembled from all their individual sculptures.

5. Once the YPE team has finished the collective sculpture, launch a discussion using the following questions:

What was it like to build this sculpture?

How was it different from only creating your own?

What does the sculpture represent to you?

Note: I like to keep this sculpture in the room throughout the process to remind the group to continue to use and build with what we have as a team.

Activity: Performing Me

Objectives

- To build the ensemble
- To explore new ways of listening and building together
- To help the YPE team stay in the moment
- To help the YPE team learn how to "not know"

Steps

1. Ask each YPE team member if he or she would be willing to do a quick performance of his or her life. Participants can do anything they want: recite a poem, sit quietly, sing, blink, dance. Each of the performances should last about one minute. Have each person think about his or her performance for a few minutes, but not for too long, as it should be spontaneous.

2. Next, have the team members go up in front of the group and perform. Have the audience applaud after each performance.

3. Once everyone has had a chance to perform, ask the YPE team to create a short play using all of the different performances.

   Note: You might want to remind everyone to listen to one another and build the play together, much as the team did during the "Yes, And . . ." game.

4. After the final play has been performed, talk to the young people about their experience of participating in it. Some of the following questions might be useful.

   What was it like to perform yourself?

   What was it like to create a play together? How did it feel?

   Were the individual characters the same or different during the individual performances and the group play? Explain your response.

   Did the group actually work together as a team to create the play? Explain your response.

   Note: The YPE team members may decide to do the play over again to practice and deepen their ensemble skills. If so, you might want to redirect the play, having the group do it in slow motion. When a play slows down, it requires that the group work more seriously on making and accepting offers. After they have done the play in slow motion, ask the YPE team to explain how this performance was similar to or different from the last one.

CREATING THE ENVIRONMENT

Early in the process of developing your YPE team, you will probably need to create some structures so that the team can operate efficiently and effectively. As always, I recommend that these structures be created in a participatory manner using creative performance techniques. Some of the structures you may want to consider creating include rules and values, roles, and monitoring tools. This section discusses each structure in detail. I am sure you will think of others as you proceed, but these should be enough to get you started.

Activity: Creating Rules

Objectives

■ To help the YPE team create a set of rules that will help the participants work as a team

■ To play with the roles of "rule maker" and "rule enforcer"

■ To help the YPE team members determine how they will monitor themselves and their work

■ To facilitate documentation of the process

■ To help individuals set both personal and YPE team roles

Steps

1. I like to begin this activity by inviting the youth to participate in a performance. Explain to the team members that they will be performing as "rule makers." Give them a few minutes to think about their performances, and tell them that at the end of that time you will say, "Action!" and that everyone will begin performing at the same time.

2. After about three minutes, say, "Action!" Everyone should perform at the same time for a minute or two. End the performance by saying, "Cut!"

3. Talk to the young people about their collective performance. You might want to use some of the following questions:

> What did the performance feel like?

> What did you notice in other people's performances?

> What are the qualities of a "rule maker"? Are these positive or negative qualities?

> If you had the opportunity both to make and enforce rules, what qualities would you like to embody?

4. Once the team members have completed their discussion, ask them to brainstorm the types of rules they would like to use in their work together. Write these rules on the flipchart. I suggest allowing the YPE team to state all of the rules first before making any edits or modifications.

PLAYING WITH THE RULES In one YPE project, the young people spent many hours creating and re-creating their rules. By the end of their efforts, the rules were very complex and strict—much stricter than any I would have proposed. They had a "three-strikes" rule: three mistakes, and you're out. They were very insistent that the group take the work seriously and that no one should have to take on the responsibilities of another participant.

One of the rules stated that the participants had to meet their work deadlines within a particular period of time. After several weeks, it became apparent that one young participant (age eight) was not keeping up with his deadlines. The group gave him one warning and then a second warning; on the third warning, the other members came to talk to me about throwing the boy off the team. They wanted me to tell him that he could no longer be part of the team because he was missing his deadlines. I told them I didn't think this was a great idea because there were extenuating circumstances with the child's school pressures and his mother. I recommended that they find a better way to handle the situation. But the young people were certain that there was no other recourse, and they wanted me to take care of it. I told them that if they were going to throw the boy out, they would have to figure out a way to do it as a group. It wasn't fair, I explained, that I, as the only adult, be the one to do it, particularly after we had spent so much time talking about my role as "adult authority figure." I also wanted to make sure that I was relating to the young people as *both* "rule makers" and "rule enforcers," taking their roles very seriously.

The YPE team agreed with me and sat together for a long time to determine how they were going to talk to the boy about his accountability to the group. When they were finished, they called the boy into the room and told him that he could no longer work with the group. It was a

5. Next, give each of the youth five red dots (or fewer, depending on the number of rules generated), and ask them to place their dots next to the five rules that they consider most important.

6. Once all members have placed their dots, have them identify which rules were most and least valued by the YPE team. Next, have them discuss whether they have differences about particular

disaster. The boy was very upset and began to cry. He left the group feeling completely rejected and heartbroken. The entire team felt terrible.

We met and talked about their performances as "rule makers" and "rule enforcers." During this long, involved meeting, we talked about how and why rules are created. We discussed the nature of rules and young people and talked about the roles of power and authority. Next, we created performances about power and authority and how they play out in the workplace. The young people were able to use these performances to take risks and go deeply into their views and beliefs about power, authority, and rule making.

After an entire day of working through this issue and playing with possible solutions and strategies, the group decided that while they wanted to take the work very seriously, they also needed to take into consideration young people's schedules, parents, and skill levels. In the end, they chose to reinstate the boy, and he was happy to rejoin the group.

This moment in the team's work, though very challenging, was key to developing the ensemble. Through all of these conversations, the young people were able to play with their understandings of power and authority in everyday life. Performance helped them explore other options for working together that they could not have previously conceived of. They came to see their rules and authority roles mirroring those of typical adults. In fact, they were not creating anything new; they were only mirroring or parroting the rules and authority roles they had seen and been subjected to. In this way, they were merely imitating adults instead of "creatively imitating them." My goal was to help them move their work closer to a creative imitation in which they could build something new. Together, they were able to create a new and different kind of working environment, one not based solely on the traditional constructs passed down to them through the generations.

rules and whether some of the rules on the list are less important than others. The YPE team may want to eliminate or revise some rules at this time.

7. Once the YPE team reaches consensus about the rules, ask members how these rules will be enforced and who will enforce them. Make sure that rules will be enforced collectively and that no single team member will bear the weight of enforcement.

Activity: Creating YPE Roles

Objectives:

■ To begin creating roles for the YPE team

■ To help the youth explore the various roles in YPE

Steps

1. Let the YPE team know that throughout any YPE process there are numerous roles to perform. Young people should be given the opportunity to play with these roles and develop them further. I like to begin by defining the various roles common in evaluation. These are some of the roles I have created with YPE teams:

> YPE team manager (makes sure that all youth attend meetings and acts as a leader within the group)

> Administrator or office manager (sets up all of the meetings, interviews, focus groups, and so on)

> Survey developer

> Interviewer

> Focus group facilitator

> Community map facilitator

> Data entry expert

> Qualitative data analyst

> Quantitative data analyst

Report or presentation writer and creator

Presenter

Notes: These are some of the common roles and responsibilities of a YPE team, but other roles may arise throughout the project and can be named along the way. Youth often develop more creative names for their roles, so by all means let them do so.

2. Before defining and explaining these roles to the youth, I ask them to create a one-minute performance of each role. Again, I have all the team members perform a given role at the same time. For example, we might have twenty data analysts in the room and twenty focus group facilitators. It is amazing how much information young people have about these kinds of roles. Without a thought, they jump immediately into these roles and accurately represent them.

3. Once they have finished, I ask team members to talk about their performances. You might find it helpful to use the following questions:

    What was the role like for you?

    Did you like or dislike it? Why or why not?

    What were the qualities of that role?

    What are the skills involved in this role?

    Was the role like you or not like you?

    Would you enjoy performing in that role or learning more about it?

    During the discussion, take notes on your flipchart. Be sure to capture the qualities and skills necessary for each role. Also, make note of the individuals who would like to explore these roles further.

Note: Be sure to clarify any misconceptions or confusion about a given role. If you don't understand the role yourself or if the group is stumped, ask someone if he or she would be willing to research the role further.

In the beginning, the young people may not have a strong sense of which roles they would like or dislike, and the YPE team will probably need to work together on most tasks. As the project grows, team members can divide the roles and responsibilities of the work

PERFORMING AS AN EVALUATOR After working with a team of young people for several weeks, I often ask them the following questions:

- How am I performing as an evaluator?

- What do you see me doing?

- What are my positive qualities?

- How do you see others relating to me?

Then I ask them if they would be willing to perform me. These performances are both extremely funny and incredibly enlightening. It is eye-opening to see how young people understand me and my role in the world. Over the years I have struggled with the fact that young people have come to see me as "old," as an "academic," and most horrifying to *my* postmodern performance, as an "evaluator." The roles these young

in any logical way. If the youth want to choose a project manager, it is especially important for them to work together for a short period of time and get to know each other before selecting an appropriate candidate.

MONITORING THE ENSEMBLE

Monitoring the YPE team helps the group document its work, reflect on its practices, and celebrate its successes. There are a number of strategies for monitoring a group's work. The ones I use include these:

- Ongoing meetings that are well documented

- Group journals or scrapbooks (including photos and drawings)

- Individual journal writing

- Individual goal setting and ongoing peer feedback

I discuss many of these strategies in this section, but you can read more about journal writing, goal setting, and scrapbooking in Chapter Ten.

people were performing were not at all part of my long-term plan, but there it is. This is how I am now seen by the youth I work with. Through these performances, I learn so much about my practice and how I relate to people. But even more important is the young people's abilities to play with my role as "adult evaluator"—creatively imitating me and simultaneously creating their own version of the "evaluator" performance.

It is difficult not to feel judged by the young people. However, they are performing only one of my roles in life. The goal of this exercise is not to make fun of the adult evaluator but to take a creative imitation approach to the characteristics we develop over the years in this profession. By doing this type of performance, young people begin to understand the qualities that they too will need to develop and those that they would like to modify. Perhaps you might see, in their performances of you, some characteristics about yourself you would like to change.

Activity: Documenting Meetings

Objectives

- To create a consistent system for communication

- To continue to create an ensemble

- To monitor the YPE team's progress and challenges

Steps

1. Hold regular meetings throughout the YPE project—a minimum of one per week. I suggest beginning each meeting by asking YPE team members to reflect on their work, particularly those activities that are going particularly well and any challenges that have come up.

2. When challenges are identified, take time to work on possible solutions.

Make sure that these meetings are well documented. You can ask one YPE team member to perform as the "note taker" during each of the sessions. I encourage the young people to take photos and write or draw these minutes in the group journal (see more about the group journal in the next activity).

Note: Documenting these meetings is important for several reasons: (1) You can follow the YPE team's progress over time, (2) the notes act as "institutional memory" so that everyone can remember the commitments made and the tasks completed, and (3) in my experience, youth love to use these notes to reflect on their process.

Activity: Group Journal Writing

Objectives

▪ To help the YPE team create a living document of its work

▪ To create an institutional memory of the team's work

▪ To develop a system to monitor progress, commitments, and completed tasks

▪ To facilitate ongoing reflection

Note: A collective journal is most often an oversized book, scrapbook, or album that can accommodate creative writing, photos, drawings, articles, and other documents. Buy one at an art supply store, and bring it in for the YPE team to use.

Steps

1. Ask the YPE team members if they would like to keep a collective journal. Show them the book, and let them know that in this type of journaling, anyone from the team can make entries at any time. When they are making entries, they can write, draw, paste in pictures, or make any other addition they please.

2. During every meeting or workshop, ask one volunteer to make a journal entry about the day.

3. Begin every new meeting by reading or reviewing the previous meeting notes and journal entries.

Note: In the beginning, no one really wants to do this. Soon, however, everyone wants to contribute something to the journal. In fact, this journal often becomes an artifact with real value in the group. YPE teams use the journal to remember and celebrate the work they have done; to document tasks, deadlines, and agreements; and to articulate their learning, contributions, and challenges.

Activity: Individual Journal Writing

Objectives

- To help the young people reflect on their own growth and change

- To generate points of discussion with the entire YPE team and possibly with a peer supervisor

- To help identify young people's strengths so that they may act as mentors or leaders of particular activities

- To identify young people's challenges so that they can be given further support

- To evaluate the YPE team's work through journaling

Steps

1. Ask the participants if they would like to keep individual journals of their work on the YPE team. Explain the purposes of keeping such a journal. If they agree, have each participant obtain a notebook to serve as a journal. (Provide the notebooks yourself if the budget permits.)

2. Talk with the team about what types of data they would like to collect in their journal. They might want to record answers to questions such as these:

   What activity did you work on today?

   Was it successful? Why or why not? What do you think accounts for that result?

   What inspired you about the work this week?

   What challenged you about the work this week?

   What contributions do you feel you made to the YPE team this week?

3. Once the YPE team members have determined a key set of questions they would like to address each week, ask everyone to write

them down on the inside cover of their journal to help them remember.

4. Ask the team members when they would like to write in their journals. Some people like to take them home and write, and some people like to have time at the end of every session.

5. Discuss when and how these journal entries will be reviewed and analyzed. Be sure to come to an agreement on which aspects of the journal will be shared and which will be private. Also, determine who will read them and when.

Note: While I think individual journal writing can be useful, I have had limited success in getting youth to do it. However, if team members are open to the idea, they might try ending each session by writing in their journals for ten minutes. One way to use the journals is to ask the YPE team members to use them as references during group meetings to talk about issues they are having trouble with and areas where they are excelling. In this way, journals are read only by the youth themselves. In some YPE teams, adult facilitators pick up journals periodically and read them. They synthesize the data and report to the group in a confidential manner so that the YPE team can deal with specific challenges. Whatever strategies you choose, make sure that the purpose of using the journals is well defined and agreed on. An important point: don't use journal writing if you aren't going to use the information for some specific purpose.

Activity: Individual Goal Setting

Objectives

- To create strategies for ongoing monitoring

- To help youth articulate and achieve their individual goals

Steps

1. At the beginning of the YPE project you may want the team members to set individual goals. To do this I like to begin by having the young people reflect on and write about the following questions:

    Why did you join the YPE team?

    What are you hoping to gain from being part of the YPE team (in terms of your emotions, practical skills, social skills, and so on)?

> What are your goals in life?
>
> How do you think this group can help you in achieving these goals?
>
> What are your goals for this project?

2. Once the YPE team has answered these questions, ask if anyone would like to read his or her journal entries aloud. Ask for volunteers. Let each person read the entries. When each person is finished reading, ask the other members of the YPE team if they can think of how they might help that person achieve his or her goals. Make sure that someone is taking notes throughout this process.

Note: If no one is willing to read aloud, ask if it would be OK for you to read the journals. If the participants agree, you can aggregate the information and give it back to the YPE team so that no individual is identified.

3. Ask the YPE team members how often they should review and reflect on their goals throughout the process. Set given times to go over these goals, and stick to the timetable. It is easy to let this activity fall by the wayside.

4. Determine who should review the goals. Does the team want to do it collectively? Does each team member want to have a partner to review goals with? Do team members want to work on their goals with the youth leader or with the adult facilitator? There are numerous choices, but once the participants have made a selection, encourage them to stick with it.

5. When reviewing goals, you might want to use the following set of questions to guide your conversation.

> Have your goals remained the same, or have they shifted? If so, how?
>
> What have you been doing to meet this goal?
>
> How much progress have you made in meeting this goal?
>
> What other supports do you need to help you meet this goal?
>
> What is your plan for meeting this goal?
>
> When do you think you will have accomplished this goal?

SUMMARY

I hope that the activities in this chapter will support you in developing your own ensemble YPE team. Creating a strong ensemble takes continuous work, so I suggest conducting some of the activities again at various points during the project. As your team progresses and begins implementing evaluation strategies, you will need to constantly remind yourself to keep the development of the ensemble in mind. Remember, the goal is to create an environment in which everyone can grow and develop. Keep pushing the boundaries around what it means to relate to and see people as *who they are becoming* rather than as who they currently are. Continue to create and re-create your role as performance director, providing numerous opportunities for your YPE team members to explore their roles as evaluators, creatively imitating and transforming not only the role of the evaluator but the methods and strategies as well. In other words, keep creating the entire evaluation play.

CHAPTER

5

DEVELOPING A YPE PLAN

When you have finished reading this chapter, you will know more about the following:

- How to work with the YPE team to create an evaluation plan that includes a logic model, an articulation of how you believe the program works, and key evaluation questions

- How to work with the YPE team to create a logic model

- How to work with the YPE team to create reality wheels so that you can collectively articulate how you believe the program works

- How to work with youth to use storyboards to help create a logic model

- How to prioritize outcomes with the YPE team

- How to work with the YPE team to create evaluation questions

Whenever I begin working with a new YPE team, I am asked the same questions: "Why do we have to do all of this planning? Why can't we just start collecting data?" I respond by saying that if you don't know what you are looking for, how can you find it? Even after many years of working in this field, I still see most evaluation teams collecting all kinds of data but using very little of it, usually because it doesn't actually answer any of their questions regarding program practices, outcomes, and impacts. In many cases, this disconnect occurs because both youth and program staff do not have a clear and shared understanding of how they should be working (methods or practices) and the results they hope to achieve. For example, the staff might not understand the program in the same way that the executive director does, and youth might not understand the program in the same way that the staff do. These different visions lead to a lack of clarity and confusion regarding both what the program should measure and how the program actually operates.

When I am first invited to work with a group of youth and staff, I review all of the materials that have been written about the program, including the Web site, the latest proposal, and any other documents. Using these materials as my basis, I create a program logic model, which is a simple description of how a program is understood to work to achieve outcomes for participants.

Much has been written about logic models and theories of change. Innovation Network (http://www.innonet.org) and Theory of Change (http://www.theoryofchange.org) are two recommended resources. The basic logic model uses a simple table (see Table 5.1) and includes inputs or resources (things needed to run the program), activities and their duration (what the program does), short-term outcomes (what happens to youth who participate for a short while), and long-term outcomes (what happens to youth who participate for a longer while). A logic model quickly reveals if the program is working—if are there enough resources to support the activities and if there are enough activities of sufficient duration to achieve both the short- and long-term outcomes.

Once I have completed a logic model for my new clients, I request a stakeholder meeting with staff, youth, program directors, the executive director, and the development officer (where applicable). During this meeting I present the logic model and ask the group to review it. The main question I ask is, "Does this look like your program?" Inevitably, the executive director and the development officer agree that this seems right. Meanwhile, the line staff and youth are mumbling to one another, saying things like "What is this?" "We don't do this," and "This isn't our program."

These opposite reactions do not mean the program is completely off track. In fact, the executive director and the development officer are doing what they do best—selling the program. The staff are doing what they do best—creating a program that meets the needs of youth. And the youth are doing what they do best—attending programs and using them

TABLE 5.1. **Logic Model.**

Inputs and Resources (what you need to run the program)	Activities and Their Duration (what the program does)	Short-Term Outcomes (what happens to youth in the program within the first six months)	Long-Term Outcomes (what happens to youth in the program longer than six months)
Example: • 15 youth leaders • $25,000 grant • 3 computers	*Example:* • Youth leaders work with 60 younger youth in 5 schools over a 2-year period, teaching them basic organizing skills. • Political action projects are developed in each school and run by the youth.	*Example:* • Youth learn basic organizing skills and terms. • Youth learn how to conduct research to support their political action.	*Example:* • Youth gain leverage in the school and are taken more seriously by the staff and administration.

for their own particular needs and ends. If an evaluation were conducted based solely on the activities and outcomes generated by upper-level management, the bigger, more realistic story about what actually happens with and for youth would be missed.

This chapter outlines some creative and playful activities you can use to plan for your YPE project. Included are techniques for articulating how your program operates, tips on how to support YPE team members to question assumptions about their program, guidelines for developing evaluation questions that will drive the YPE project, and strategies for selecting evaluation methods. Each activity can be used on its own or in conjunction with any of the others.

ASKING FOR WHAT YOU WANT If you are still not convinced that evaluation planning is important, let me tell you another story. Recently, an arts program called me in a panic. The administrators had been collecting data for some time, and their evaluation consultant had left them high and dry. They needed someone to take the data and analyze them. They were desperate, so I agreed. They shipped me a large box full of raw data, and a colleague and I started analyzing. After hours of interpreting the data, we realized that we had very little to say about the program's impact on youth. I called the executive director and asked what the organization was hoping the data would tell them. It became clear that they would never get the answers to their questions using the data they had collected. I quickly requested a stakeholder

---

ARTICULATING HOW YOUR PROGRAM OPERATES

To evaluate your program, you must first be able to articulate how you think it works. I generally rely on three activities to do this: Reality Wheels, Storyboards, and Logic Modeling. These activities can be used separately or in conjunction with one another.

Activity: Reality Wheel

Objectives

■ To help program members articulate their program model

■ To clarify program goals

■ To identify possible short- and long-term program outcomes

■ To facilitate a discussion about what might be missing in the current logic model

Steps

1. On a large flipchart, draw a giant wheel: one large circle with a small circle in the center.

2. Ask the YPE team to think of the program's goals. A goal is generally much larger and broader than a single outcome for participants.

meeting with all staff members to create a logic model. After a full day's work, the group produced a logic model that represented the relevant program activities and outcomes. We then looked back at the instruments currently being used and discovered that they were not capturing data about any of the projected outcomes.

This was a very expensive lesson. The moral of the story? Do not measure things just because you can. Create a plan for your evaluation that clearly states the questions you want to answer about how your program operates or the program outcomes and impacts. Make sure that these outcomes and impacts are closely aligned with what your program does. For example, don't measure increases in school grades if you do not provide youth with academic support.

It is generally something that will happen to participants over a long period of time. This goal should be tied to the program mission—for example, "Economic security for all young women in the Bedford Stuyvesant neighborhood of Brooklyn."

3. Put this long-term goal in the center of the wheel—for example, "Youth in East Harlem are able to realize their dreams" or "Young sex workers are able to live a healthy lifestyle."

4. Collectively define all of the institutions and groups that influence this long-term goal. For example, if the center of the circle is "Homeless girls in Los Angeles have happy, healthy homes," then institutions that influence this outcome would include the legal system, the girls' families or lack thereof, the shelter system, schools or the lack thereof, the health care system, and so forth. Jot down each of these institutions on the flipchart.

5. When the group members have exhausted their list, ask them to determine the degree to which each of these institutions affects the goal. For example, the legal system might have a big impact on the youth while parents and families have little influence because the young people do not have contact with them. As the YPE team determines these levels of influence, create "slices" of the wheel for each institution in proportion to its degree of impact. Label

each "slice" appropriately. Have the group continue to refine the wheel until you have the proportions correctly represented.

6. Next, have the YPE team shade the "slices" according to the degree to which their program has worked to influence that particular institution, group of people, network, policy, and so forth. For example, if the group agrees that its program has worked primarily with schools and parents, shade these two "slices" of the wheel with the greatest amount of color, starting from the center outward.

7. Use the data generated from this wheel to discuss the following questions:

> Do you think that the program is going to be able to reach its long-term goal?

> Do you think the program's activities are having the greatest impact they can have on this community? If so, why? If not, why not?

> Do you think this program is headed in the best direction it could take? If so, why? If not, why not?

> What areas do you think you need to work on?

Note: Take notes during this conversation either on the flipchart or in the group journal. Point up any issues and questions concerning the direction of the program's activities, populations served, partner organizations, and impact areas. This conversation can help the team develop interesting evaluation questions that the youth can examine throughout their YPE project.

Activity: Storyboard

Objectives

- To understand more clearly how the YPE team members think their program works to achieve its goals and objectives

- To help youth define their program's populations, activities, and short- and long-term outcomes

Note: During this activity, YPE team members can work in teams or individually.

REALITY CHECK
I worked with a program that had identified the long-term goal of helping young people in East Harlem realize their dreams. However, after completing the Reality Wheel exercise, the administrators realized they were focusing all of their attention on high school completion rates and college enrollment. This was only one small piece of the pie, and it became clear to them that they would never obtain their long-term goal of helping youth realize their dreams unless they refocused their work and the ways in which they evaluated it.

Another program I worked with had the long-term goal of producing young community organizers and activists. This organization had a long history of accomplishing this goal, but it was beginning to realize that while the youth in its programs were terrific community organizers, they were not completing high school and were ending up in dead-end jobs. When we began working on their Reality Wheel, staff and youth identified the long-term goal of "Supporting the development of young people so that they can be successful in life." This shift in focus allowed them appropriately to define all the influences in the community that affect this goal, such as education, healthy living skills, the arts, and organizing and activism. Prior to creating new programs, they met with the young people and had an open dialogue about these new ideas and garnered their support and ideas for future changes.

Steps

1. Hand out three 12-by-14-inch sheets of poster paper to each individual or team. Ask team members to develop a story about how a young person might move through the program.

    Board 1: Ask each team to draw a visual representation of the young people prior to coming to the program. Who are they? What are their issues and challenges? Why do they come? How do they hear about the program?

    Board 2: Ask each team to draw or write about what happens to a young person after entering the program. What do newcomers hear, see, feel, touch? What activities do they participate in? What changes occur for them individually (in knowledge, skills, behaviors, attitudes), in their social networks, in their communities, and so forth.

Board 3: Ask each team to create a visual representation of what happens to a young person after leaving the program. What challenges do "alumni" face? What choices do they make as a result of having been in the program?

2. When the drawings are completed, have each individual or team present its story to the group. Have someone take notes on the flipchart. I recommend placing four sheets of flipchart paper on the wall, respectively titled "Population Served," "Program Activities," "Short-Term Outcomes," and "Long-Term Outcomes."

Population Served: As each team discusses Board 1, write down all of the information given about the young people who come into the program. How old are they? Why did they come to the program? Where do they live?

Program Activities: As each team discusses Board 2, note all program activities that the groups report being important to young people and what kinds of relationships seem key (with adults, with youth).

Short-Term Outcomes: As each group discusses Board 2, also note all the short-term outcomes (things that happen to youth while they are in the program). What do they say happened to them while they were in the program (changes in perspectives, new friends, new types of relationships with adults, learning new skills, and so on)?

Long-Term Outcomes: As each person relates his or her story from Board 3, note all of the long-term outcomes expressed. What happens to youth when they leave the program? How have they changed or grown?

3. Talk with the team about the similarities and differences in their drawings. Use the following questions to spur conversation:

Does every team member see the program in the same way? Why or why not?

What are the similarities and differences in each of the stories?

Do all young people in the program have similar experiences or different ones? Explain your response.

How long do young people have to stay in the program to have the experience you describe?

4. Hang these pictures on the wall if you wish so that all members of the YPE team can study them more carefully later.

Note: Another variation on this exercise is to have different groups in the organization, such as staff members, board members, parents, and community members, draw their versions of this story. It is interesting to see if there are variations in how each of the different stakeholders sees and understands the program. This exercise is a great way to begin a logic model and gather data about the organization and its outcomes. Think about using this activity during a focus group.

A TALE OF TWO PROGRAMS?   While working

with an arts-based community organizing and activist group in the Bronx, New York, I asked group members to do the Storyboard exercise. The adults worked together to complete a visual representation of their program, and the youth worked separately to create their own. The adults' pictures illustrated young people in their program going out into the community to create social change. The youth's pictures showed young people coming together to learn new job skills and gain support from peers and adults. At the end of the process, the two groups shared their drawings with one another. The staff members were shocked to realize that the youth had a totally different understanding of the program. The youth and the staff spent many hours talking about these differences. It turned out that the adults had not done a good job of communicating with the youth about the community organizing and social change model. The young people did not understand that the activities provided by the program were related to social change. This process led the group to work closely with the youth to devise new activities that more specifically mirrored their understandings of social change.

Activity: Logic Modeling

Objectives

- To create a simple description of how a program is understood to work to achieve outcomes for participants

- To help the YPE team and other stakeholders gain a shared understanding and vision about the program (in other words, to get everyone on the same page)

Note: Logic models can be created by the YPE team alone or in concert with other program stakeholders such as staff, board members, administrators, development officers, fundraisers, and funders. It is important to invite both stakeholders who know a lot about the program being evaluated and stakeholders who need to learn more about the program. For example, the development officer may know very little about the day-to-day operations of the program but could benefit from more information to improve his or her capacities as a grant writer.

You may choose to have one large stakeholder meeting that includes both the YPE team and all of the other stakeholders. Or you may hold one meeting with the YPE team first and then a second meeting with other stakeholders (such as parents, community members, or board members). If you choose the latter, begin the stakeholder meeting with the YPE team's logic model and ask for feedback and critique.

Either way, this activity is lengthy, and I often conduct it during two separate three-hour-long stakeholder meetings. If time is at a premium, you may choose to rate only the outcomes and not the activities.

Steps

1. If you have already conducted the Storyboard exercise, you have a terrific list of "activities," "short-term outcomes," and "long-term outcomes." Prior to beginning the Logic Modeling activity, consolidate all of the outcomes provided by the various youth (and where possible other stakeholders). Group similar outcomes together, or combine them accordingly to eliminate duplication. Typically, the list will contain both outcomes (what happens to a participant in your program as a result of your activities) and indicators (how I know a result has been achieved—what I can determine through my senses). To the degree possible, group the indicators underneath the outcomes to which they correspond. Don't forget that indicators describe outcomes and that there can be more than one indicator

per outcome. For example, if one outcome is "increased leadership skills," the indicators might include "ability to speak out about an issue," "the skills necessary to organize a project," "self-confidence," and "caring." The outcome of "increased literacy" might be defined by indicators such as "youth read more books," "youth are more excited about going to the library," and "youth score higher on a reading test." List all of these points on a flipchart so that they can be used during your stakeholder meeting.

2. Review the list of activities you developed during the Storyboard exercise, and make a clean list. Again, group and regroup them until there is a logical order and similar activities are placed next to one another.

3. Explain to the members of the YPE team (and stakeholders) that a logic model is a simple "picture" of how their program operates to achieve its outcomes. The logic model will help them identify outcomes that are closely related to the activities they do in the program. There are many different kinds of logic models and many ways of creating them, but the basic components include these:

   Inputs or resources—what the program needs to operate.

   Activities—what the program does and for how long.

   Outcomes—changes in behaviors, skills, knowledge, attitudes, condition, or status.

   Indicators—specific, measurable characteristics or changes that represent achievement of an outcome. They are how you know the outcome is happening. Indicators are directly related to the outcome and help define it. Indicators are specific.

4. Begin by reviewing the list of outcomes with the group to see if there is anything missing. Be sure to add any outcomes or indicators the group identifies. Again, be sure to put these new outcomes or indicators close to similar ones on the list. If the members of this group were not involved in the Storyboard activity, let them know how this information was generated. Be sure to post the list where everyone can see it before you begin.

5. Once the outcome list is finalized, ask the YPE team (and stakeholders) to rate them. Give each of the participants five red sticky dots, and ask them to place the dots next to the outcomes they think are the most important for the program.

6. After everyone has rated the outcomes, conduct a quick analysis of the findings. Count the number of dots next to each outcome, and talk about the findings. For example, "increased literacy" may have been rated as the most important outcome (seven out of nine participants gave it a dot). Be sure to note the numbers next to the outcomes on the flipchart. Discuss the outcomes that have the highest consistency and those that have little consistency. Ask the participants if these findings seem right to them. Are these the outcomes that are most important to them overall? Talk to the group about these outcomes, and determine if these are really the most important outcomes or if they might be indicators of something else.

7. Next, give each of the participants five green dots, and ask them to place the dots next to the outcomes they believe the program is best at achieving.

8. Once they have finished, conduct a quick tally, and report the findings to the group. On the flipchart make note of the items that were identified as very important but were not seen as being achieved by the program, and vice versa. Take time to discuss any findings in the data that seem particularly interesting.

9. After all the outcomes have been rated, move on to the list of activities created during the Storyboard activity. Ask the group to review the list of activities to see if any are missing and if so, add them to the list.

Note: If you are holding only one stakeholder meeting, you may not have time to proceed to Step 10, rating the program activities. In that case, you may want to simply make a list of these activities and ask the group if all of the key activities are on the list.

10. Give each of the participants five blue dots, and ask them to place the dots next to the activities that are "the most popular."

11. After they have rated the activities, conduct a quick analysis of the findings. Count the number of dots next to each activity. Make note of these on the flipchart. Talk with the group about the findings, specifically the activities with the highest number of red dots. Ask the participants why they believe these are the most popular activities.

12. Give each of the participants five yellow dots, and ask them to place the dots next to the activities they believe are "best at supporting their key outcomes."

13. After they have rated the activities, count the number of yellow dots next to each activity. Make note of these on the flipchart. Talk with the participants about the activities with the highest number of dots. Ask why they believe these activities are the best at supporting their key outcomes. Note the differences and similarities in the activities the group rated "popular" and those rated "best at supporting key outcomes," and discuss these results. For example, you may need to ask why the participants thought one activity was extremely important to achieving their outcomes but was not at all popular with the youth or others involved.

14. Ask the group to tell you about all of the resources available to the program—staff, computers, grants, volunteers, and so forth. Write these on the flipchart.

15. End the stakeholder meeting here, telling the group that you will come back with your notes and a draft of the logic model.

16. Use all of the information you've collected to create a logic model: line up the flipchart pages with the headings "Inputs," "Activities," "Outcomes," and "Indicators," and create a table that matches the data.

17. Once you have revised the logic model and put it in table format, distribute copies to all stakeholders in the group. If possible, have another meeting, and ask the group to answer the following questions:

> Does this program make sense?
>
> Are there enough resources to run the activities? Why or why not?
>
> Are there enough activities to achieve the outcomes? Why or why not?
>
> How long would a young person need to be in the program for the most important outcome to occur?
>
> Are the activities the appropriate ones to achieve the outcomes?

Note: Beyond their usefulness in evaluation, logic models should also serve as communication tools about the program and how it operates. Therefore, it is important that the model make sense to anyone who picks it up. The group might also want to share its logic model with "supportive others" to see if they think it is a fair representation of the program and the way it works to achieve its outcomes.

WHAT ARE YOU TALKING ABOUT? While working with a youth drug prevention program in Canada, I found that the youth and the adults had very different ideas about how the program operated and what its outcomes should be so we had the youth and the adults work together to create a logic model of their program. We asked both the adults and the young people to rate the outcomes that they believed were most important for the program to accomplish. The adults rated "decreases in drug use" as the most important outcome, while the youth rated "improved relationships with family members" as the most important outcome. The staff had no idea that the program was helping young people achieve better relationships at home. The youth, for their part, were unaware that they were enrolled in a "drug prevention program." This activity revealed an entirely new vision of what the program was all about.

FORMULATING EVALUATION QUESTIONS

Asking questions may seem like an easy enough task, but when you actually have to do it, thinking of appropriate questions can be difficult. In particular, young people often have difficulty performing as "question askers" because in most environments they are considered "dumb" for asking questions. Instead, they need to perform as "knowers" or "question answerers." Switching from the performance of "knower" to "questioner" is not so easy. As noted in Chapter One, I often use "question asking" performances to create environments in which youth are truly comfortable asking question without knowing the answers. My favorite performances generally employ the roles of scientist, anthropologist, or explorer. In these types of performances it seems perfectly natural and acceptable to ask questions and explore possible answers. In this section, I offer a set of activities for coming up with appropriate evaluation questions.

Activity: Question-Asking Performance

Objectives

- To help YPE team members ask questions about their program

■ To come up with a short set of questions that will help guide the evaluation process

■ To clarify what the evaluation will explore and what it will not explore

Steps

1. Let the members of the YPE team know that to conduct a strong evaluation, they need to become good "question askers." Just like most scientists, evaluators need to be very curious and ask lots of good questions.

2. Ask the team members to imagine that they are anthropologists or scientists who have just landed on Mars and have met a new intelligent life form. What types of questions would the anthropologist or scientist ask? Have them list every possible question they can imagine.

3. Ask the YPE team to pick one or two questions to explore further.

4. Once the team has selected its questions, ask what the anthropologist or scientist would need to do to explore these questions further. What strategies or tools would the adventurer have to develop to answer the team's questions? What would the person specifically be looking for? What might the person decide to exclude from his or her exploration?

5. When the team is finished with this performance, talk with team members about the importance of formulating evaluation questions that will drive their YPE project. Evaluation questions, like the questions in their performances, define both what will be examined throughout the evaluation process and what will not. Developing good evaluation questions is very important because the questions they ask will drive the answers they get. Explain that good evaluation questions should have the following characteristics:

> Questions should be complex enough to elicit rich data but should not be so complex that people have difficulty understanding them.

> Questions should have more than one possible answer.

Answers to the questions should not be predetermined by the way they are worded.

Askers should not be able to answer the questions themselves.

Questions should address issues that are useful to the program.

Askers should gather data from people with different perspectives.

Questions should address aspects of the program about which data can be gathered (in other words, don't ask about the outcomes for alumni if you can't reach most of them).

Questions should address aspects of the program that can be changed.

Baker & Sabo (2004); modified from the Bruner Foundation.

6. Ask the members of the YPE team to continue their question-asking performance, but this time to perform in their roles as evaluators who are studying their program. As they perform in these roles, have all participants shout out questions they would like answered regarding aspects of their program—how it operates or the effect it has on its beneficiaries.

7. Once the team members have exhausted their questions, explain to them that it is most effective if the study focuses on one or two questions. This close focus makes the study easier to manage. To select the best questions, begin by grouping similar questions together. Ask the team if there are questions that are similar enough to be consolidated into a single question.

8. After grouping the questions, the team can either vote on the questions or use sticky dots. If you use sticky dots, give each of the participants two dots, and ask them to place the dots next to the questions they consider the most important.

9. Count up the dots to see which questions were considered most important to the group. Take some time to discuss why these questions were chosen while others were not.

10. Once the YPE team has decided on its one or two most important questions, have the team review them to make sure that they fit the criteria listed in Step 5.

11. Let the YPE team know that these questions will now drive the rest of the evaluation effort. The goal now is to determine the best methods and strategies for exploring these questions.

THE QUESTION-ASKING GAME Asking questions can be very difficult for youth evaluators. When I am working with a program to develop evaluation questions, I might ask the members of the group to imagine that they are famous scientists and have invented the newest cutting-edge technology for music, such as an iPod or the CD. I have them imagine themselves in this role and think about all the questions they would need to ask in order to develop this invention. I ask the participants to shout out their questions as they think of them. They might ask, "How can I fit the most music in the smallest amount of space?" "How can I carry all of my music with me wherever I go?" "How can I download music from the Internet?" In other words, I engage them in a question-asking activity.

After they exhaust all of their questions, I ask the young people to imagine that they are social scientists trying to invent the most effective program for youth. I invite them to think about the types of questions they would ask as this kind of scientist. The group may shout out questions like "What do young people want?" "What do youth need?" and "What programs already exist for youth?"

After the young people have been engaged in asking questions for a few minutes, I might say, "OK, now you are famous evaluators coming to look at this program. What questions would you want to ask about the program?" Once they are involved in this question-asking activity, it is much easier for them to develop questions about their own practices. At some point they realize, "Hey, I can ask questions. This isn't so tough" or "It's OK to ask questions; even the most esteemed scientists in the world do it." This type of imaginary play is often very helpful because it supports youth and adults to engage in an activity before knowing how to do it. They are not stopping themselves from participating in the belief that they do not know how to or are incapable of doing it.

CHAPTER

6

TRAINING YOUNG PEOPLE AS INTERVIEWERS

When you have finished reading this chapter, you will know more about the following:

■ The definition of an interview and a rationale for conducting one

■ How to work with the YPE team to create interview guides or protocols

■ How to work with the YPE team to gain permission from the respondents to be interviewed

■ How to work with the YPE team to select interviewers and respondents

■ The roles of interviewer and note taker

■ How to work with the YPE team to perform as interviewers

A youth-led interview of an adult is powerful because the relationship between them can be radically transformed through the interview process. As noted earlier, youth rarely have the opportunity to perform as "question askers"; instead, they are relegated to answering the questions of adults. When youth become the interviewers, adults often have a very different experience of youth and their capabilities. From this new perspective, youth often experience both themselves and the adults they are interviewing very differently.

PERFORMING AS AN INTERVIEWER While working with a group of young journalists who were covering a United Nations General Assembly special session, one nine-year-old journalist on our team bumped into Secretary-General Kofi Annan. She got so excited that she ran right up to him and asked him for an interview. He was shocked—he looked down at her and then up at his colleague as if to ask, "What am I supposed to do?" While he was trying to come up with a gentle way to turn her down, she followed him into the elevator and asked him once again for an interview. Admiring her persistence, he agreed to grant her a private interview later that week. She developed a fantastic interview protocol and worked with others in the group to hone her interview skills. She went to the interview well prepared and with a very professional attitude and demeanor. The secretary-general responded in kind by being remarkably candid and respectful.

During this interview, the two roles of "nine-year-old interviewer" and "leader of the international community" began to dissolve, and what remained was a very unique performance of two people communicating and relating to one another on equal terms.

This chapter will explore multiple strategies for helping young people perform as effective interviewers. Many books have been written on interviewing, so I do not cover all the basics here. Instead, you will find some unique and creative interviewing strategies that can be used with youth.

Activity: What Is an Interview, and Why Should I Conduct One?

Objectives

■ To introduce the YPE team to interviewing methods

■ To help the YPE team develop appropriate interview questions

■ To teach the YPE team how to select respondents
■ To teach the YPE team how to conduct different types of interviews

Steps

1. When talking with young people about interviewing, I often use the following definition: "An interview is a one-sided conversation between an interviewer and a 'respondent.' Interview questions are most often determined prior to the interview and recorded on what is called the interview protocol. The purpose of an interview is to discover another person's perspective about a particular issue (the person's own growth and development, the program, the community, and so on). During interviews, information can be gathered about the respondent's feelings, thoughts, intentions, and behaviors."

2. Let the YPE team know that interviews are particularly useful in the following circumstances:

    If you have a small group of people (no more than two dozen) whose opinions you want to understand, you can arrange to interview them all.

    If you have a large group of people (more than two dozen) whose opinions you want to understand, you can interview a smaller, representative group of these people—what is called a sample.

    If you want to create a strong survey, start by conducting a few interviews. Through interviews you can learn more about the language that the group uses and design instruments that make sense to the respondents.

    After you have conducted a survey, you can interview some of the respondents to gain a deeper understanding of the responses. For example, if you discovered through a survey that most youth in the program don't like its leadership training aspects, you can interview some young people to find out why.

3. Next, ask YPE team members to go home and watch their favorite talk show hosts to examine their interview styles. Or ask them to

recall some of their favorite talk show hosts. Specifically, have them watch for (or recall) some of the following characteristics:

If the interviewers let the audience know what their positions are on the topics or if they keep their opinions to themselves

If the interviewers are really listening to the respondents and building a conversation or if they simply have a set of questions they are trying to run through

If the interviewers stay neutral no matter what the interviewees tell them

If the interviews are one-sided conversations or a back-and-forth exchange of views and ideas

4. Once they have reviewed interviewing styles, talk to the YPE team about a specific type of interview that is nonjudgmental and that allows the respondent to express opinions without interference from the interviewer. This type of interview is used most often in evaluation and in most social sciences.

    Let participants know that in this type of performance the interviewer is "curious," "fascinated," and "radically accepting." Ask the group to recall the "Yes, And . . . " activity in Chapter Four and remember how they had to truly listen to one another without judgment.

Note: You might play the "Yes, And . . . " game again to help the group remember the feeling of giving and accepting offers.

5. Set aside a few minutes for a short improvisation of an interview with the YPE team. Have team members perform "curious and fascinated" for one minute.

6. When they have completed this short improvisation, talk to the young people about their performance. Ask them the following questions:

    What was the performance like?

    How was it different from a regular conversation?

Did you listen differently? If so, how?

Did you move your bodies differently? If so, how?

Activity: Creating Interview Guides or Protocols

Objectives

- To create a set of questions (guides or protocols) to use while conducting an interview

- To help the YPE team members align the questions in their interview guide with their evaluation questions and their logic models

Steps

1. Inform the members of the YPE team that they have produced several aids that can help them with developing appropriate interview questions. These aids include the evaluation questions and the logic model (see the Logic Modeling activity in Chapter Five).

2. Post the evaluation questions on a flipchart, and hand out copies of the logic model so that the YPE team can review it.

3. Have the YPE team members examine the list of indicators on their logic model and let them know that this list can help them to come up with interview questions. For example, if one of their outcomes is "increased leadership" and indicators are "speaks out within the group" and "knows how to take actions in the community," interviewers might develop questions that will help them understand if a given young person has these attributes. Here are some possible questions:

   Can you describe yourself? (*Probe or follow-up question:* Are you quiet? Outspoken? Shy?) Please give an example.

   When you are working in a group, do you generally share your opinions and thoughts? If so, can you give an example? If not, why not?

   What issues have you most recently spoken out about within a group? Where did this take place? Who were you with?

   Have you ever organized a group to take action on an issue? Is so, can you describe this project? If not, what would you do to organize a group of people to take action?

4. Have the YPE team members brainstorm all of the questions they would like to ask and note them on the flipchart.

5. Once the YPE team has exhausted its list, begin to group similar questions together, arranging them in a coherent order. This is often a difficult task. Here are a couple of tips:

    > Begin the interview with some simple questions that are easily answered. For example, "What is your name?" "How old are you?" "How long have you been coming to this program?" Then get more specific as the interview proceeds.

    > Be sure to develop probes for questions when needed. A probe is a follow-up question that helps when a respondent is having difficulty answering a question. For example, if you ask the question "What was your life like when you first started this program?" you might need to follow up with some probes, such as "How old were you?" "What school were you attending?" or "What grade were you in?"

    > As you are ordering the questions, stop periodically and test them out by interviewing another member of the team. Keep doing this until it seems that there is a logical order to the questions and that they flow easily for both the interviewer and the respondent.

6. Inform the YPE team that at the beginning of every interview protocol, there should be a short paragraph explaining the purpose and focus of the interview and what will be done with the data collected when all the interviews are finished (see Exhibit 6.1). This paragraph should give information about the confidentiality of the interview. In most cases, the people being interviewed should be assured that their names will remain confidential and will not be attached to any quotes or specific findings. This paragraph should also explain how the interviewers plan to record the interview, how they will ask permission to tape-record or videotape the interview, and that if respondents sign waivers to permit their images to be used, the interview will no longer be confidential. Also, respondents should be informed of the approximate amount of time the interview will take.

7. Spend some time with the YPE team to develop this opening script for your evaluation protocol.

EXHIBIT 6.1. **Introduction to an Interview**

Social Change Program Staff Interview Protocol
October 2008

Hello, my name is _____. We are conducting an evaluation of _____
_____ (name of program). We really want to understand how staff
members in social change programs are supported to develop as professionals and individuals. The goal of this study is to help programs improve
and deepen their staff development strategies. Our conversation will be
completely confidential. Your name will not be used in relationship with
these data. We will be reporting our findings to the _____ (name of
foundation), and we will be happy to send you a copy of our final report.
The interview should take us approximately 20 minutes to complete. If
there are any questions that you do not want to answer, you don't have
to. You can also stop the interview at any time. Do I have your permission
to begin the interview?

8. Work with the team to practice performing this script. As the team
members perform the script, you can make revisions as necessary
so that everyone feels that the wording is as strong as possible.

Activity: Selecting Interviewer Respondents

Objectives

- To help the YPE team determine whom to interview

- To ensure that respondents are representative of the entire population

Steps

1. If the YPE team has not already done so, facilitate a discussion
about the types of people the group would like to interview (for
example, parents, youth, teachers).

2. Once the team has created an exhaustive list, ask the following
questions:

Why do you want to interview these types of people?

What perspective does this group of people bring to the table?

Is it important for the perspectives of a variety of groups to be captured in order to address the evaluation questions?

Can some types of people help address certain questions and not others?

If so, what types of questions should be asked of which types of respondents?

3. Let the members of the team know that if there are more than two dozen people in a particular group, they might not be able to interview everyone. In this case, they will need to select a "sample" to interview.

4. Explain that a sample is a small group of people whose perspectives and views should represent or mirror the larger group's perspectives and views. Therefore, it is very important to think deeply about the different types of people the YPE team needs to hear from in order to get the whole story.

5. Have the YPE team members think about all of the different types of people in each of the groups they want to interview. Have them create a list of differences that may exist within these groups. For example, if they want to interview a sample of youth in the program, factors to consider might include these:

Age

Gender

Grade in school

What school they are from

How long they have been in the program

Their position in the program or the types of activities they have been involved with

6. After you have listed all of the different variables, work with the YPE team to determine a representative sample of people within the group to interview. Explain to the YPE team that "representative" means that the voices of the people being interviewed will represent all of the voices in a given group.

TABLE 6.1. **Population Details for Selecting Respondents.**

Age Range	9–11	12–15	16–18	19–21
Number of Young People	5 males	12 males	10 males	2 males
	1 female	13 females	20 females	5 females

Note: You might find it useful to create a table similar to Table 6.1 to help you understand the population more fully. This type of table will help you determine the number of people to interview so that you can be most certain that the data are representative of the entire group.

Try to select individuals who fit a wide range of these characteristics. For example, to ensure proper representation from the population depicted in Table 6.1, you might select two youth between nine and eleven, one male and one female (even though this is not proportionally accurate, it is important to hear the perspectives of both genders); six youth between twelve and fifteen, three males and three females; eight youth between sixteen and eighteen, five female and three male; and three youth between nineteen and twenty-one, one male and two female.

Activity: Matching YPE Team Interviewers with Respondents

Objectives

- To help match the appropriate YPE team interviewer with the right respondent

- To give young people a positive interviewing experience

- To ensure that respondents are comfortable answering questions

Note: Depending on the nature of your study, making appropriate matches of YPE team members and interviewees can be challenging. This is especially so when interviews are conducted with peers or with particularly difficult adult authority figures. Following are some helpful hints to think about when matching YPE team members with their prospective respondents. Review them once the YPE team has decided on both the population and the specific individuals to be interviewed.

Tips for Matching YPE Team Members with Other Youth Respondents

1. It is often difficult to interview a close friend or peer. Match interviewers with young people they are less familiar with.

2. It can be difficult if a YPE team member already has some preconceived negative feelings about a particular potential respondent. When matching interviewers and respondents, these questions can be helpful: "Do you think that you can conduct a fair and objective interview with this person?" "Do you think your past relationship and feelings about the person will color your interview?" If the YPE team member feels there might be a problem, match the person with someone else.

3. Continue to work hard on YPE team members' performances in the roles of "professional evaluator" and "interviewer." Have the young people rehearse their performances multiple times before they conduct the real interview.

4. Only YPE team members who are comfortable and ready to conduct interviews should participate in asking questions. There are other roles for those who are less confident or enthusiastic about this task.

Tips for Matching YPE Team Members with Adult Respondents

1. YPE team members may have some preconceived thoughts and feelings about some of the adults they are going to interview. When matching youth with adults, be sure to ask the same types of questions suggested in Tip 2 for youth respondents.

2. Conduct the following Performing as an Interviewer activity, and make sure the team is given multiple opportunities to conduct interviews with "difficult adults." In other words, arrange for interviewing performances in which young people learn to deal with all types of adults.

Activity: Performing as an Interviewer

Objectives

■ To support the YPE team members as they practice their roles as interviewers

■ To play with the notion of what it means to be an interviewer

■ To allow YPE team members to evolve their own unique interview styles

■ To provide youth with opportunities to develop strategies to deal with difficult respondents

Steps

1. Go over the interviewing tips in Appendix A with the YPE team.

2. Ask the YPE team to split into three groups. One group will perform as "interviewers," one group will perform as "note takers," and one group will perform as "respondents."

3. Next, split the interviewers and note takers into pairs.

4. Using the interview protocol the YPE team has created, direct the note takers and the interviewers to talk for a few minutes to set up their interview performances.

5. While the interviewers and note takers are working together, invite the respondents to talk with you in a separate group. Explain to the members of this group that you would like to help them with their performances as respondents. Let them know that you want to provide the interviewers with some very different types of challenges. Therefore, you would like the respondents to take on certain characteristics, such as "talkative"; "terse, giving one-word answers"; "annoyed"; "busy"; "evasive, going off on tangents and avoiding answering the question directly." Feel free to add any other characteristics that may seem realistic or relevant.

Note: Do not let the interviewers know you are giving these roles to the respondents.

6. Determine which respondents will be matched with which interviewers or note takers, and send them over to the appropriate part of the room to begin their performances.

7. Have them begin their interviews. During this first attempt, give them only about ten minutes to work on their performances. (They can use the protocol developed in the Creating Interview Guides or Protocols activity earlier in this chapter.)

8. When the ten minutes are up, talk about the experience. Ask the following questions:

    How far did you get into the protocol?

    What was the interview like?

    Was it a one-sided conversation?

    Were you able to move the interview along at the pace you had hoped for?

    What challenges did you encounter?

    Were you able to really listen to the responses?

    Did you come up with follow-up questions that were not on the protocol?

    Did you remember to use probes when the respondent got stuck on a question?

    Was the note taker able to capture all that the respondent was saying?

9. Next, allow everyone to conduct the interview again, and ask the respondents to be much more cooperative this time.

10. After they have finished, ask the questions in Step 8 again.

11. Next, switch roles so that everyone gets a chance to be respondent, interviewer, and note taker. After each performance, give the YPE team members an opportunity come back together as a group to talk about their experiences. Ask the questions in Step 8 to each new set of interviewers.

CHAPTER

7

TRAINING YOUNG PEOPLE AS CREATIVE FOCUS GROUP FACILITATORS

When you have finished reading this chapter, you will know more about the following:

■ What a focus group is

■ The value of using focus groups

■ How to work with the YPE team to develop focus group protocols

■ Creative activities that can be used during focus groups

■ How to work with the YPE team to select focus group participants

■ How to work with the YPE team to conduct a focus group

■ How to work with the YPE team to perform as focus group facilitators

Conducting focus groups is a terrific method for gathering data because you can be very creative and support participants to "think outside

THE SQUEAKY WHEEL GETS THE OIL

I once worked with a group of young people to run a focus group with parents. The executives and staff believed that the parents were generally unhappy with the quality of the program. The youth were not so sure about this. Together we selected a group of parents to participate in a focus group. Two members of the group were known to have challenges with the program, and the other members were selected at random. During the focus group it became apparent that the two parents who did not like the program were alone in their views and that their experiences were unique and highly specific. In fact, the real issue was not the quality of the program but several bad exchanges the two parents had had with staff. By the end of the focus group, the participants had developed recommendations based on all of the parents' experiences and views of the program rather than on the complaints of a disgruntled few.

the box." Focus groups are especially valuable when trying to understand complex issues and develop recommendations for change.

This chapter outlines a number of unique performatory and playful focus group activities that can be done with any type of respondent (youth or adult). If you would like to learn more about focus groups, many books on the subject are available, particularly in the field of marketing. Tips for conducting focus groups with youth can be found in Appendix B of this book. An excellent online resource is the Free Management Library, which has a specific section on focus groups (`http://www.managementhelp.org/evaluatn/focusgrp.htm`).

Focus groups can support the members of the group to think outside the box, stretching and developing their perspectives. Focus groups have the potential to be ZPD-rich environments in which participants learn from one another. Instead of trying to capture the view of each individual person within the group, the purpose of the focus group is to capture the views and dialogue of the entire group.

In the first part of this chapter I share some strategies for helping YPE teams conduct focus groups. Six activities cover the following topics:

- Defining focus groups and why to conduct them

- Developing focus group protocols

- Setting up the focus group

- Selecting focus group participants

- Identifying various roles in focus groups

- Conducting focus groups

In the second part of the chapter I present four creative activities that can be that can be used to help focus group facilitators establish unique dialogues with participants. Depending on the issue, the YPE team can use any number of these activities to help facilitate focus groups. The following activities are covered:

- Word association

- Collage and drawing

- Community mapping

- Imagining the organization as a movie

HELPING YOUNG PEOPLE CONDUCT FOCUS GROUPS

Activity: What Is a Focus Group, and Why Should I Conduct One?

Objectives

- To introduce the YPE team to focus group methodology

- To help the YPE team develop questions for focus groups

- To help the YPE team select participants for focus groups

- To discuss the various roles involved in focus groups

- To help team members play the roles of focus group facilitator, note taker, and observer.

Steps

1. Talk with the YPE team about focus groups and how they differ from interviews. I like to use the following script:

   Focus groups are generally conducted with small groups of people (no more than twelve and no fewer than four). During focus groups the respondents are asked to discuss a particular topic or topics that have been announced in advance. This activity differs from interviews in that you are not interested in each individual's perspective. Instead, the *discussion* provides the data. In other words, it is important that the members of the group shape each other's thinking throughout the process. The data you are gathering are not so much the thoughts and feelings that the individuals bring to the group but rather the thoughts, feelings, and perspectives that the group develops together.

2. Review the advantages and disadvantages of focus groups with the YPE team. I often use the points listed in Table 7.1.

TABLE 7.1. Advantages and Disadvantages of Focus Groups.

Advantages of Focus Groups	Disadvantages of Focus Groups
• Focus groups foster the collection of deep, rich data about the group members' shared and differing thoughts or feelings about an issue or topic.	• To develop a strong focus group, participants must be chosen carefully (small groups of either very similar individuals or very different individuals).
• Focus groups promote an understanding of the ways in which individuals are influenced by one another.	• Focus groups are difficult to run if there are too many conflicting opinions.
• Focus groups allow participants to remind each other of events or issues that individuals might not have thought of on their own.	• Focus group data are difficult to analyze and summarize.
• Focus groups provide an opportunity for people to talk and think more deeply about an issue.	• Focus groups are not effective for exploring individuals' views and perspectives.
• Focus groups help build trust among the members.	
• Focus groups promote a deeper understanding of perspectives and viewpoints.	
• Focus groups help participants begin developing recommendations and solutions.	

Baker & Sabo (2004); modified from the Bruner Foundation.

Activity: Developing Focus Group Guides or Protocols

Objectives

■ To create a set of questions (guide or protocol) for the YPE team to use while conducting a focus group

■ To help the YPE team members align the questions in their focus group guide or protocol with their evaluation questions and logic model

Steps

1. Let the YPE team know that like interviews, focus groups need a protocol or guide. These protocols ask a variety of questions or introduce a variety of issues. A focus group protocol is less structured than an interview protocol and has fewer questions in order to allow time for the entire group to discuss each issue. A focus group should take one to two hours and requires careful preparation.

2. Inform the members of the YPE team that they have created several aids that can help them develop a focus group protocol. These include their evaluation questions and their logic model.

3. Post the evaluation questions on a flipchart, and hand out copies of the logic model so that the YPE team can review it.

4. Have the YPE team members examine the list of outcomes and indicators on the logic model and let them know that this list can help them develop focus group questions or general themes to explore. For example, what do respondents think are the most important activities, impacts, and outcomes of the program?

5. Have the YPE team members brainstorm all of the questions and issues they would like to explore and post them on a flipchart.

Note: Have the team members begin thinking about the types of issues they would like to address with a focus group. However, do not finalize the protocol until after you have read through the remaining activities in this section of the chapter. You may be able to use one or more of them to guide your discussion. As you review the following activities with the YPE team, think about how each might spark the focus group participants' thinking. You may even want to try a few with the YPE team to see how they work.

6. When the YPE team members have exhausted their list, begin to group similar questions and themes together, arranging them in a coherent order. The following tips can help with this often difficult task:

> Begin the focus group with very simple, direct questions that almost anyone can answer. I like to use the First Thing You Think Of activity (in the second part of this chapter), which allows participants to get into the swing of answering questions and helps them feel that they can participate.

> Be sure to develop probes for questions when needed. A probe is a follow-up question that is often helpful when the group seems stuck or quiet. For example, if you ask, "What do you think youth gain from being in this program?" you may need to follow up with some probes, such as "Do you think they learned anything new? If so, what?" or "Do you think they acquired new skills? If so, what skills in particular?"

7. Inform the YPE team that at the beginning of every focus group the facilitator should explain the purpose of the focus session and what will be done with the data when the session is finished. The facilitator should also provide some explanation about confidentiality, letting the participants know that their names will remain confidential and will not be attached to any quotes or specific findings. Facilitators will also need to say something about how they plan to record the focus group, how they plan to ask for permission to tape-record, and how long the focus session will last.

8. Spend some time with the YPE team to develop the opening script for its evaluation protocol.

9. Work with the team to practice performing the script. As the youth perform the script, make any necessary revisions so that everyone feels that the wording is the best possible.

Activity: Selecting Focus Group Respondents

Objectives

■ To help the YPE team determine whom to engage in the focus group

■ To help the group determine the number of focus groups that should be held

Steps

1. If the YPE team has not already done so, facilitate a discussion about the types of people the group would like to include in the focus session or sessions (for example, parents, youth, or teachers).

2. Once the team has created an exhaustive list, ask the following questions:

> Why do you want to include these types of people?
>
> What perspective does this group of people bring to the table?
>
> Is it important for a variety of perspectives to be captured in order to address the evaluation questions?
>
> Can some types of people help address certain questions and not others?
>
> If so, what types of questions should be asked of which types of respondents?
>
> Can these groups of people be in the same focus group, or will there need to be more than one group for each type of participant?

3. Explain that the recommended number of people per group is six to ten. Depending on the project, the YPE team may need to hold only one focus group; sometimes it may be preferable to have several focus groups with either very similar or very different participants (for example, different age groups of youth, parents, staff, politicians, and so on). It is not easy to identify the most appropriate participants for a focus group. If the group is too different, in terms of age, class, or gender, the differences can have a considerable impact on the group's ability to participate and share ideas. Alternatively, if the group is too similar, the range of opinions and experiences expressed during the discussions may be too narrow. One rule of thumb is that participants need to feel comfortable with one another. A second rule of thumb is that participants should be representative of the entire group in terms of gender, class, ethnicity, length of time in the program, and so forth.

4. Work with the YPE team to determine the most appropriate number of focus groups and the best possible participants for each group. It might be useful to develop a table similar to the one we used in Chapter Six for selecting interview respondents (see Table 6.1).

Have the YPE team think of the different types of people within each group and then create a list of differences or variables that exist within the group. For example:

Age

Gender

Grade in school

What school they are from

How long they have been in the program, their position in the program, or the types of activities they have been involved with

5. After you have listed all of the different variables, work with the YPE team to determine a representative sample of people to invite to participate in the focus group. Try to select individuals who exhibit a wide range of characteristics.

6. Now it is time to invite the various participants to join the group. With people being so busy nowadays, scheduling a focus group requires careful planning, so advise the YPE team to allow enough time to set up the groups. When team members contact potential participants, they should let each one know the purpose of the focus group, how the data will be used, where the session will take place, and how long the meeting will take (this information should appear in the introduction to the protocol).

7. Work with the YPE team to find an appropriate space for the focus session. The space should be quiet enough that conversations can be easily recorded without a lot of external noise and private enough that participants have some degree of anonymity.

Activity: Conducting a Focus Group

Objectives

- To help YPE team members perform as facilitators, note takers, and observers

- To help them become proficient in their roles

Note: This activity is more effective once you have had the opportunity to engage the YPE team in some of the creative group activities in the second part of this chapter.

Steps

1. Explain to the YPE team that there are three different roles in focus groups: "facilitator," "note taker," and "observer." See Appendix B for tips explaining each role. Go over these roles with the YPE team.

2. Determine which of the YPE team members will perform as facilitators, observers, or note takers. You will also need a few people to perform as focus group participants. (If there are not enough team members, you may need to invite some other young people to perform in these roles.) You can ask for volunteers for the various roles, or you can allow each team member to try out each role for a few minutes.

3. Give each of the YPE team members a few minutes to research and practice their roles and prepare for their performances.

4. When the youth feel they are ready, begin the focus group performance.

   Note: You can either allow the performances to continue throughout the entire focus group protocol, or you can switch roles every five minutes or so. In this way, each young person will have the opportunity to perform in the various roles.

5. When the performance is finished, ask the team members how they thought the focus group went. Here are some questions to facilitate the conversation:

   What went really well during the performance?

   What needed some improvement?

   Was the note taker able to keep up with the conversation?

   What did the observer note about the group?

   Are there any redirections that could help improve the performance?

CREATIVE GROUP AND FOCUS GROUP ACTIVITIES

Activity: The First Thing You Think of When I Say . . .

Objective

- To get the group warmed up and talking to one another

■ To help group members feel comfortable answering questions

■ To gain information about the group's perspectives, views, and feelings about the issue or subject your are studying or evaluating

Steps

1. Keeping the specific issue that you are exploring in mind, begin the focus group by asking questions that everyone can easily answer, such as "What is the first thing you think of when I say (name of this town)." Begin with topics or issues that are general and not necessarily related to your question or topic. Note the responses on a flipchart.

Note: In the following steps you will be asking the respondents how and if they see a relationship between the broader topic you have chosen and the narrower subject you are exploring. For example, one YPE team I worked with asked the youth to begin by shouting out the types of things they most like to do in their free time. Later they asked the types of things they liked doing in their program. Then they were asked to compare the two lists to determine where they were similar and where they were different.

2. Once participants have shouted out answers, I ask a question more related to the issue but still fairly general. For example, I might ask, "What is the first thing you think of when I say (name of school or after-school site)?" Continue to note responses on the flipchart.

3. Once they have exhausted their responses, I move even closer to the issue by asking, for example, "What is the first thing you think of when I say (name of program)?"

4. Once they have finished responding, I ask the YPE team to look at all of the lists created and find any similarities between the (name of town) and the program or between program and school or between town and school. In other words, how are the items on the lists similar or different?

Note: This activity often leads to some very interesting comments or new ways of thinking about the program that have not been considered before. Leave the notes up during the remainder of the focus group so that people can refer to them.

Activity: Collage and Drawing

Objectives

■ To elicit deep and rich information about the group's experiences, feelings, thoughts, and views

■ To help the group engage in thoughtful conversations about the drawings

■ To help group members reflect on their personal experiences and create visual representations of them

Note: This work can be very emotional, eliciting information about participants' deepest feelings. I have had focus groups create visual representations of the following:

> Young people's experiences of school
>
> Young people's experiences of the program
>
> A new, improved reality for youth—the "dream"
>
> What a typical drug user looks like
>
> What a typical youth looks like in this community
>
> How a young person comes into the program
>
> How social change happens
>
> What group members believe happens to a young person in the program
>
> Who young people are before they come into the program; how they choose to participate; what happens to them when they join; what changes occur in their lives because of their participation; and who they become in the world

Steps

1. Work with the group to determine the best subject for a collage or drawing activity. This will depend on the type of information you are hoping to gather.

2. Purchase art supplies such as markers, glue, and stickers. Gather magazines, newspapers, and other materials with a broad range of images.

3. Place all of these materials on tables, and ask the participants to work for about twenty minutes to create their individual collages or drawings.

4. When they are finished with their visual representations, ask participants to present their collages to one another. Have them talk about why they selected key images and phrases. As they talk, jot down key points on a flipchart.

5. Follow up by asking some of these questions:

> Why did you choose these specific images?
>
> What do they represent for you?
>
> How does your picture feel to you?
>
> Did you learn anything while you were creating your representation?

6. After each participant has had the opportunity to speak, go over the notes you have taken, and ask follow-up questions such as these:

> In what ways are your visual representations similar? Different?
>
> What are the key themes that came up in each collage or drawing?
>
> What were the positives and negatives?

7. Talk to the group members about the items on the collages and drawings that point to a new direction for the future. Ask how these solutions might work in their specific communities.

What Does It Look Like? During one project when I was working with groups of youth from around the world, I wanted to know more about how they understood drug use in their communities. I asked the group to name all of the drugs that were used most often in their communities and wrote them all down. Once we had created this list, I asked the group members to draw pictures (or find photos in magazines) of typical people who used these drugs. The collages and drawings the young people produced were remarkable. Some young people from South America represented cocaine users by drawing farmers with green teeth, while youth from Great Britain represented cocaine users as upper-middle-class, very thin young women. These drawings continued to provide much discussion about what it meant to be a "drug user" in each of the various countries represented.

Activity: Mapping

Objectives

- To understand the group's experiences of space and relationships

- To help the group gain a rich understanding of issues of access, proximity, feelings, perspectives, local behaviors, and activity settings

Note: Mapping can be done in a variety of ways. Participants may produce flat maps, small-scale models, and maps made with sticks and dirt. Maps can be created in fairly large groups or individually. I have had focus group participants create maps of the following places:

> *Their communities*—marking places where they interacted with other youth, where their program was located, where dangerous activities took place, where safe places existed. With this particular group, I was looking at the location of the program with respect to "dangers in the community" and how the program was dealing with these dangers.

> *The places where they grew up*—where they played, hung out, felt safe, learned, had friends, and so on. With one particular group, I wanted to learn more about how adult staff members had grown up and their relationships to their communities. These maps were then compared to the maps the youth in the program had created.

> *Their townships*—schools, community-based organizations, where undocumented youth lived, and where youth hung out. This information was used to highlight the various types of activities available to youth in the community and became a base map for an outreach effort that attempted to engage a broad range of young people.

Steps

1. To begin a mapping activity, the group or the individuals must create a "base map." A base map generally includes key features of the community such as landmarks, main streets, churches, parks, and schools.

2. Next, different aspects of the community or environment can be noted. For example, you might want participants to indicate where their houses and schools are, where children play, where drug activity

takes place, where they feel the safest, where they learn the most, and so forth. Be sure to create a list of all landmarks you would like them to highlight. I often hand out colored dots so that participants can mark each type of landmark with a different-colored dot.

3. After participants have finished their maps, ask for volunteers to share their maps with the group. Take notes on a flipchart.

4. When all participants have shared their maps, ask the following questions:

What similarities or differences do you see in our maps?

Why might these exist?

How might our experiences and relationship to "community" differ?

Which Community Is Ours? I once worked with
a group of adult staff members who were trying desperately to support youth to engage in community organizing. I asked the adults to draw a map of where they had lived during their adolescence. The adult maps were fascinating. It turned out that during their adolescence they had spent most of their time participating in activities outside of their local communities (dance troupes, theaters, schools, environmental movements, and so on). During the mapping activity, the adults began to talk about their sense of community when they were young as being very separate from their geographical location. Light bulbs went off! What if the youth they were working with felt similarly about their communities? What if the youth wanted to have experiences outside of their communities more than they wanted to change their current communities? The staff decided to conduct the same mapping activity with the youth to learn their perspectives on the community.

Another key point came from this activity: the adults recognized that they could not even have thought about making changes within their communities before gaining new perspectives. These new perspectives had come from their experiences outside of the community. As a result, the staff realized the importance of supporting youth in getting out of their communities to gain new experiences and perspectives.

Activity: If This Organization Were a Movie . . .

Objectives

- To gain understanding of the group's experiences of a program, organization, company, group, team, relationship, or the like

- To help group members think and talk about their work together in new ways

(See page 27 for discussion.)

Steps

1. Ask the group members to think about their program or organization and come up with a movie title that best sums up their work. For example, one youth group I worked with came up with the title *Its All About the Kids,* and another selected *School Invaders.*

2. Once the group's "film" has a title, ask the group members the genre their movie would fit into: science fiction, soap opera, horror flick, and so on. The group can shout out answers while you write them on a flipchart.

3. Next, ask the participants to decide who the stars of the movie should be.

4. Have them identify which supporting roles would need to be case.

5. After the various roles in the organization have been identified, ask the group to decide who should play each of these characters and why.

6. Once the group has figured cast the movie, ask them to write a brief script and act out a one- or two-minute performance.

CHAPTER

WORKING WITH YOUNG PEOPLE TO DEVELOP SURVEYS

When you have finished reading this chapter, you will know more about the following:

■ The definition of a survey

■ The value of using surveys

■ How to work with the YPE team to create a survey

■ How to work with the YPE team to select survey respondents

■ Creative survey strategies, including human surveys, candy surveys, and sticker surveys

Surveys are among the most misunderstood data collection methods. Everyone hates them, but they are used more than any other method because they are easy to create—or so everyone thinks! In my experience, surveys are one of the most difficult evaluation methods. They are hard to create because the designer has to develop questions and answers (or the response categories) and write both in a language that is understandable to the audience.

MAKING SURVEY QUESTIONS MEANING-FUL TO YOUTH
I worked with a group of young people who ran a reproductive health program for youth. They decided to create a survey but kept writing surveys that I felt were inappropriate, asking questions and coming up with response categories that seemed illogical and occasionally demeaning. In addition, I thought the youth they were surveying would not answer the questions truthfully because they were too personal. After many hours of going over the survey questions, one young man said to me, "Look, we have been talking to youth about these issues for many years. Trust us, these are the kinds of things they typically tell us." I decided to trust them; they administered the survey to the youth in their

In working with a YPE team, I often recommend that a number of interviews be conducted prior to creating a survey. For example, if a YPE team wants to conduct a survey with youth in its program, I may recommend that the team members interview five or six participants prior to developing the survey instrument. Interviewing prior to creating a survey supports a stronger understanding of the types of questions that will work with your population. Interviewing also gives you access to the language people use to express themselves. Armed with this new information, it is easier to develop appropriate, understandable questions and response categories.

Rather than cover everything about conducting and administering surveys, this chapter focuses on strategies for good survey design and administration as well as several creative survey methods. The first part covers a number of survey tips and topics, including these:

■ What is a survey and why should I do one?

■ Creating surveys

■ Selecting survey respondents

In the second part of the chapter, I present some creative performatory activities that can be used with a YPE team or with other stakeholder groups:

■ The Human Survey

■ Candy surveys

■ Sticker and sticky dot surveys

program, and we had a 100 percent response rate—every young person filled out every question. The response categories that had challenged me seemed completely reasonable to these youth. It just goes to show how much power there is in understanding your audience before you create a survey. There is no way that I, as a professional evaluator, could have created that survey. There is also no way that I, as a middle-aged adult, could have administered it. I am certain that if I had been the one to hand out the survey, I would have encountered much more resistance. The youth who administered the survey were peers; therefore, the respondents had a completely different reaction to the questions.

HINTS FOR CREATING AND ADMINISTERING SURVEYS

Activity: What Is a Survey, and Why Should I Conduct One?

Objectives

■ To introduce the YPE team to survey methodology

■ To help the YPE team create survey instruments

■ To help team members select respondents for their surveys

Steps

1. Talk with the YPE team about the definition of a survey. I like to use the following script as a guideline:

> Surveys generally include a series of questions with predetermined response choices. These response choices can be lists of items (for example, "Which of the following activities have you participated in? Mark all that apply."); they can be scales ("Rate the following statements from one to five, five being the best" or "Indicate how much you like something: 'not at all,' 'somewhat,' or 'a lot'"); or they can be simple "yes" or "no" responses.
>
> Surveys can also include some "open-ended" questions that allow the person responding to write in an answer, using his or her own words. Surveys can be completed either by a respondent or by the person giving the survey. [Baker & Sabo, 2004; modified from the Bruner Foundation]

Only use surveys when you have a large population (more than twenty-five or thirty people). With a smaller group, interviewing can be just as effective, if not more so, because you can obtain more specific information. However, if the data you are using are very sensitive, you may want to use a survey to protect the respondents' anonymity.

2. Review some of the advantages and disadvantages of using surveys with the YPE team; these are listed in Table 8.1.

TABLE 8.1. **Advantages and Disadvantages of Surveys.**

Advantages of Surveys	Disadvantages of Surveys
• Easy to quantify (count up) and summarize results • Useful when trying to collect data from large groups • Good for studying attitudes and perceptions • Good for studying self-reported behavior changes • Good for collecting sensitive data that should be confidential or anonymous	• Difficult to create because they rely on language that is clear, concise, and understandable by respondents • Impersonal • Often difficult to use with young children or people struggling with literacy issues (more creative approaches like those in the second part of this chapter can work)

Baker & Sabo (2004); modified from the Bruner Foundation.

Activity: Developing a Survey

Objective

■ To help the YPE team develop an effective survey instrument

Steps

1. Have the YPE team conduct some online research to explore the various types of surveys. In particular, have them find answers to the following questions:

How are the surveys designed? Is the layout user-friendly?

What are the response categories that people use?

What types of demographic data are requested (age, gender, ethnicity, and so on)?

Are there any questions on these surveys that you could use on your survey?

2. Have the group members talk about the various instruments they found. Ask them to identify their favorite surveys and the specific questions they liked best.

3. Have the YPE team members brainstorm the types of questions and key themes they would like to cover on their survey. Remind them that they have already created several aids that can help them with this task, including their evaluation questions and their logic model (see the Logic Modeling activity in Chapter Five). The logic model is a helpful reminder of the outcomes and indicators they are hoping to explore. Note the questions on a flipchart.

4. When the brainstorming on key questions and themes is done, ask the team to go back and revise the questions, ensuring they meet the following criteria:

    The questions are clear and specific.

    Each question asks only one question.

    The questions elicit all necessary information, including basic descriptive data (age, ethnicity, gender, length of time in program, specific group, and so on).

5. Once the questions have been decided on, the team will need to develop response categories. Response categories can be phrases or lists. For example, "a lot," "a little," "some," and "not at all" are common phrase response categories. Or if you ask the question "What activities have you participated in?" your survey can provide a list of activities conducted in the program for respondents to check off. Have the YPE team work through each question and determine the best responses for each. Be sure to include directions for each response ("Mark all that apply," "Mark only one answer," "Explain your response," and so on).

6. Next, work with the YPE team to arrange the questions in a logical order. I recommend starting with demographic information, but

this may not be the best strategy with your given group. Often it is best to begin with the most general questions and work toward more specific questions as the survey proceeds.

7. Work with the YPE team to develop a survey introduction. This short paragraph should explain the purpose and focus of the study. It should also include information about what will be done with the data when the survey is finished, how long the survey will take to fill out, and what the respondents should do with the survey after they have filled it out. The introduction should also state whether or not the survey is confidential or anonymous. Whatever the case, respondents should be assured that their names will not be used in any way in connection with the data.

8. Once the members of the YPE team have completed the final draft of the survey, they can pilot-test it. Select a small group of people (representative of the people you want to survey in terms of age, gender, and other aspects) to complete the survey. Tell the respondents that the YPE team wants to find out if they think the survey works as it should. Therefore, you want them to indicate questions they have trouble understanding, response categories that they think are odd, and any other problems they encounter in taking the survey.

9. Time the respondents as they fill out the survey. This will allow you to know approximately how long the survey will take a respondent to complete.

10. When the respondents have finished filling out the surveys, ask the YPE team to interview them about their experiences. The following questions can be used:

    Did you understand all of the questions? Were they asked clearly, using language you would use?

    Were there any questions that were difficult for you to answer? Which ones? Why were they difficult?

    Were the response categories provided ones that you were comfortable with?

    Did you feel the urge to write in information to answer or qualify a particular question? Which ones? Why?

11. Use this feedback to refine the survey before using it.

Activity: Selecting People to Survey

Objectives

- To help the YPE team determine to whom to administer the survey

- To help determine the likely number of survey responses that can be obtained

Steps

1. If the YPE team members have not already done so, lead a discussion about the types of people they would like to survey (parents, youth, teachers, and so on).

2. Let the YPE team know that when conducting surveys, it is often impossible to include everyone because there are simply too many people to survey. When this is the case, you might want to survey a smaller group that will represent the whole. This is usually called a representative sample. Creating these kinds of samples can be extremely complicated, and you might need a bit of help.

   Note: See Appendix C for help in figuring out an appropriate sample size. If you are interested in understanding more about how to select a sample, I encourage you to read one of the many books on the subject. The key to sampling is that *more* is not always *better*. In other words, creating a representative sample means targeting the right group of people whose responses will likely mirror those of your entire population. This is why in election exit poles, for instance, so few responses are needed to reveal the voting patterns of the entire state or nation quite accurately. The trick is selecting the right group, not increasing the number of respondents. One rule regarding sampling is that if your population is fewer than one hundred, you should try to get surveys back from all respondents.

3. Work with the YPE team to determine the most appropriate types of people to survey. Have the team members think about all of the different types of people in each of the groups. Have them create a list of differences that may exist in the groups, including these:

   Age

   Gender

   Grade

What school they are from

How long they have been in the program

Their position in the program or the types of activities they have been involved with

4. After you have listed all of the different variables, work with the YPE team to determine a representative sample of people to survey. Try to select individuals with a wide range of characteristics.

5. Now it is time to administer your survey. Explain to the team that there are a variety of ways to administer a survey, including face to face, by mail, on the telephone, and via the Internet. Each approach has pros and cons. Review these with the YPE team members to determine the best way to administer their survey.

Administering Surveys Face to Face. Because you have a captive audience, administering surveys in person is the best strategy for getting satisfactory responses from a large percentage of the selected survey population (this is known as a "high return rate," highly desirable in surveys).

If you are going to administer a survey in person, explain the purpose of the survey, and ask the group members if they would be willing to participate.

Selecting the person who hands out the survey is very important. The respondents should trust this person and believe that their data will be kept confidential.

Administering the Survey by Mail. Mail surveys often have a very low return rate because people put them aside and then lose them or forget to fill them out and send them in by the cutoff date. If you feel that a mail survey is the only way to go, be sure to allot time to remind the respondents to fill it out. You may even want to devise a way to know who has and has not filled it out so that you can focus on those who have not. If you are going to administer a survey by mail, make sure that the introduction is very clear and concise so there is no miscommunication about how the data will be used.

Administering the Survey on the Telephone. Phone interviews can be very useful when dealing with populations that respond well to personal interaction. They are time-consuming, however, because it takes many phone calls before you will reach someone who agrees to answer the survey. Selecting the person to administer the survey is very important.

Be sure the person is someone who comes across as trustworthy and objective.

Administering the Survey via the Internet. Internet surveys can be terrific if the selected respondents have access to and know how to use e-mail. These surveys are often very user-friendly and can be customized with color and photos. Internet surveys eliminate the need for a data entry process because the participants enter their data directly into an online database.

CREATIVE APPROACHES TO SURVEYING

Two excellent examples of creative surveys are the Human Survey activity in Chapter Four, "Developing the Ensemble YPE Team," and the Logic Modeling activity in Chapter Five, "Developing a YPE Plan." The Human Survey activity, sticky dot surveys, and candy surveys can be used with your YPE team or any stakeholder group as an alternative to paper-and-pencil surveys. The thing to remember about nontraditional approaches to surveying is that you can be as creative as you like. You can use candy, flash cards, sticky dots, jelly beans, whatever you think will work with your group. These types of nonwritten surveys are especially suitable for use with groups of respondents that have low levels of literacy or who are burned out on the paper-and-pencil test-taking mode of providing feedback.

Activity: Human Surveys

Objective

- To help the group develop a creative, interactive survey with the people in a room

Steps

1. Prior to conducting a human survey, the team members will need to develop a protocol, or a set of questions, to ask the respondents. They will also need to determine response categories for each question. For example, the response categories for "How true is this statement?" could go from "very true" to "not at all true"; or if the survey is ranking how much the participants enjoy

SURVEY GAMES
A colleague and I were given the daunting task of working with youth from thirty-three countries to evaluate their thirty-three different drug prevention programs. The youth spoke six different languages, and many of them were street children with limited literacy. But these were not the only challenges; the budget only allowed for us to travel to one of the programs. At first we thought this was an impossible task. After a long debate about whether we were crazy to take such a job, we decided to develop a creative game that would act as a type of survey. What we developed was a series of game boards for youth to fill out. To play the game, the youth would need to conduct

---

various activities, the response categories could go from "very enjoyable" to "not at all enjoyable."

2. Once the team members have defined their questions, create an imaginary line in the room; for example, pick a chair at one end (point A) and a door at the other (point B). Make point A one end of the response categories (for example, "absolutely true") and point B the other (for example, "not at all true"). Go through each item on the protocol one at a time, and have the participants position themselves on the imaginary line to reflect where they fit on the continuum.

3. Once they have chosen their places for an item, ask a few participants why they are standing in that particular spot. Try to get answers from those standing at each point along the line.

4. After participants have explained why they have chosen their particular position on the line, ask the group some of the following questions:

    How is this group similar?

    How is this group different?

    Are people all standing in the same place for the same reasons or for different reasons? Why has this happened?

Note: One group member can ask the questions and another can document the results. On a flipchart, note how many participants are standing in which locations. On another page, jot down the qualitative

some research in their communities and in their programs. As the youth discovered the answers to the game questions, they would fill out the boards and then move on to the next stage. Each program received a large box with all of the materials necessary for each group to play the game and conduct research. Each box included cameras, pencils, sticky dots, markers, a video, and giant workshop boards. As the youth gathered information, they filled out the game boards, marking their responses with sticky dots and drawings, and provided information in other creative ways. Essentially, these game boards served as very large interactive surveys.

responses that participants make about why they are standing where they are on their Human Survey response line.

Activity: Candy Surveys

Objectives

- To help the group create a creative, fun survey that can be eaten

- To design a fairly anonymous survey

Steps

1. Before conducting a candy survey, the group will need to develop a protocol, or set of questions, as well as response categories for each question. I usually limit the number of questions on candy surveys to five or six.

2. Have the group write each question in very large print on a sheet of standard 8½-by-11-inch paper. The questions can be posted outside a classroom, workshop room, or wherever the group meets. This allows the respondents to have some privacy when they are responding to the survey. This is particularly important if the survey is about the quality of the training or about the facilitator's approach.

3. Next, code the response categories to match the colors of the candies (or candy wrappers) you will be using. (Use individually wrapped candies that can be safely eaten after handling.) For example, the red candy could represent "very true" or "very

enthusiastic" or "learned a lot"; the green candy could represent "somewhat true" or "somewhat enthusiastic" or "learned some"; the yellow candy could represent "not at all true" or "not at all enthusiastic" or "learned nothing."

4. Place an empty bucket or other container next to or below each posted question.

5. Make bowls of individually colored candy available so that participants can easily select the corresponding color from the bowls.

6. Ask the participants to take the survey using their candy. They should answer each question by taking a piece of candy that matches the answer they've chosen and dropping it into the bucket. For example, if "very true" is color-coded red, and the respondent wants to choose that answer, the person should drop a red candy in the bucket.

7. Once everyone has had the chance to complete the survey, count up the number of different colored candies per question.

8. Ask the participants to refrain from eating the candy until after they have taken the survey. Also, make sure they do not eat candy from the bowls that are holding the survey responses.

Note: Much like candy, stickers and sticky dots of multiple colors can be used to represent different response categories. Different-shaped stickers such as smiley faces and stars can also be used. Sticker surveys are great when working with very small children. They like to keep the leftover stickers after the survey work is completed.

Stickers can also be used for rating activities. This method was used in the Logic Modeling activity in Chapter Five and is highly effective with other types of stakeholders. If you are interested in this approach to surveying, go back and review the process, mirroring it with different groups. In particular, having various stakeholders rate the importance of particular outcomes can be extremely valuable.

Let the members of the YPE team know that they should be as creative as they like with these types of surveys. Almost anything can be used to represent a response category or a rating, so feel free to use objects that are meaningful to the populations you are working with.

STUCK ON STICKER SURVEYS When I was conducting a sticker survey with young people in Bolivia, they let me know that they really enjoyed the process. They were very careful to use each sticker conservatively and placed each exactly where it belonged. It was a "collective" survey, so the group discussed and debated each response carefully. I thought this behavior was very interesting; they almost seemed to be saving the dots. At the end of the survey, they gathered up all of the stickers and put them back neatly in their packages. As we were leaving, one small child handed the packages of stickers to me. I told him that he and the others could have the stickers to keep. I have never seen a group of children so excited. Within minutes they had stickers all over their bodies—from head to toe. Even the small donkey that accompanied them was not exempt from the sticker mania. This image of ten small children and a donkey covered in stickers is a favorite memory and is only one testament to how much children enjoy these kinds of surveys. But sticker mania is not limited to youth! I also have stories of adults turning immediately childlike when the stickers were presented and becoming equally joyful about the survey process. For evaluators, this is a big deal. After all, when is the last time you saw anyone get excited about filling out a survey?

CHAPTER

USING PERFORMANCE AS A DATA COLLECTION STRATEGY

When you have finished reading this chapter, you will know more about the following:

■ The definition of performance and how it can be used as an evaluation method

■ The value of using performance in evaluation

■ How to work with the YPE team to create improvisations that can generate data

■ How to work with the YPE team to select performance participants

■ How to work with the YPE team to perform as directors of data collection performances

The first eight chapters of this book have covered using performance as a developmental activity. In this chapter I discuss how to use performance to collect data. I am sure you won't be surprised to learn

STAFF PERFORMING AS PARENTS During one meeting with an after-school program, it became apparent that the staff did not have very high opinions of the parents. No one could really articulate what the problem was, but everyone knew there was a problem. I asked the staff to break into smaller groups and prepare short performances of typical encounters with parents. They worked on their performances for about ten minutes, and then we all came back together. Each group was asked to perform its parent encounter for the larger group. After all of the performances were completed, we realized that one particular theme kept coming up. The younger staff members were getting bullied by parents, and they were not able to respond quickly enough to the parents' demands. Once we identified the major challenge, the more experienced staff members talked to the younger teachers about other possible performances they could have when parents approached them in a bullying manner. Together, the group members directed and redirected their performances until they began to get more satisfactory results from those who were playing the parents. This data collection moment turned into a professional development opportunity. Furthermore, it led to a recommendation to continue this type of professional development with all of the teachers.

that performance is one of my favorite data collection methods! With performance, you never really know what is going to happen. Performance provides a different avenue for communication, one that is not so reality-based. While performing, people end up sharing all types of information. There are some things that we can say or communicate during play that we can't (or wouldn't) in everyday life.

Some of the topics this chapter covers include defining and using the performance method, creating improvisations, selecting performance participants, and performing as directors.

Activity: What Is the Performance Method, and Why Should I Use It?

Objectives

- To help the YPE team understand how to use performance as a data collection method

■ To help the team create performance protocols

Steps

1. Discuss what performance means with the members of the YPE team. Brainstorm with them about their views and understandings of performance.

2. Share with them the following definition of performance:

   Performance is an activity that helps people play with concepts, feelings, viewpoints, roles, and characteristics. It is a unique data collection strategy because it encourages respondents to go beyond their conversational understanding of a given subject. During performances, participants are required to use their physical and emotional powers to create something, and in doing so they often glean new understandings and gather new strategies for expressing themselves about a given matter. In this way performance moves beyond dialogue, allowing expression to unfold through movement and the senses.

3. Ask the YPE team members if they can think of ways they might like to use performance as a data collection tool in their YPE project. Brainstorm possibilities and scenarios in which performance might be useful to elicit more meaningful responses to their evaluation questions. You may want to post the evaluation questions on flipchart pages and hand out copies of the logic model for the YPE team to review (see the Logic Modeling activity in Chapter Five). During the discussion, record the possibilities and scenarios on a flipchart.

   Note: Here are some examples of performance scenarios:

   A typical performance of a young person before coming into the program, while in the program, and after leaving the program

   A typical youth (or group of youth) in a particular school

   A typical youth at school and a typical youth in your program

   A typical youth-adult relationship in a particular school

   A typical youth-adult relationship in your program

4. Determine one or two issues, characteristics, perspectives, or scenes that you would like to understand more fully through performance.

Activity: Creating Improvisations

Objectives

■ To teach the YPE team how to create performances in order to collect data

■ To help the team direct these performances

■ To help the team document the data generated during the performances

Steps

1. Begin with the one or two issues or scenarios the YPE team developed in the What Is the Performance Method activity.

2. Ask the YPE team the following questions:

   Who are all of the characters that typically participate in this type of scenario (younger children, adults, parents, community members, older youth, and so on)?

   What are each character's main goals or objectives in the scene? Why? What are the motivators?

   What are the roles and characteristics of each of these different characters?

   How do each of the characters perceive and feel about one another?

   What do we need to further understand about this scene and the characters in it?

   How will understanding this scene help us address our evaluation questions?

3. Record the YPE teams' answers on a flipchart.

4. As you brainstorm these questions, more issues that you may want to explore will likely arise.

5. Work with the YPE team to create two or three scenes for the actors to perform—for example, a youth and an adult trying to make decisions together in the program about a specific issue or two young people from different schools trying to work on a project together.

6. To test how these scenes might work, the YPE team can perform them.

7. Once the team members have determined the most appropriate scene, work with them to develop an introduction and directions for the respondents they will be working with. In other words, they might say, "In this performance exercise we would like you first to convey a really horrible partnership between youth and adults. In the next scene we would like you to depict a really good partnership between youth and adults."

8. Also work with the YPE team to develop one or two possible ways to redirect the action once the first performance is done—for example, "Now that you have completed those two scenes, we would like to see them again in slow motion" or "Now that you have completed those scenes, perform it again with the adult facilitator speaking Spanish" or "Repeat the scene with the adult facilitator exaggerating his or her manner of listening" or "It seems that there are three main types of characters in this scene—the intellectual, the moneybags, and the dumb student. Can we take these roles even further?" This type of redirection helps exaggerate or intensify the issue, yielding even greater insights.

9. Remind the YPE team that you will need to conduct some "warm-up" exercises with the actors before beginning the performances. Recall some of the activities you have done earlier, such as the "Yes, And . . ." game, Performing Me, and My Gift to the Group (all in Chapter Four). Also, have everyone think of other fun games that might help the group warm up.

10. Once the team members have brainstormed the games, have them choose one to use during their performance activity.

11. Work with them to create a script that they can use to introduce the performance activity to the actors they will be inviting to perform. This introduction should briefly describe the YPE project and explain that they are using these performances as a data collection

tool. Be sure to say something about why you are conducting this study and how the data will be used, and inform them that they will receive a summary of the work they do.

Activity: Selecting Performers to Participate

Objectives

■ To help the YPE team decide whom to invite to perform

■ To help the group determine the number of performance groups to conduct

Steps

1. If the members of the YPE team have not already done so, lead a discussion with them about the types of people they would like to include in the performances.

2. Once the group has created an exhaustive list, ask the following questions:

    Why these types of people?

    What information might we gain from them?

    Is it important for each of these different perspectives to be captured in order to address the evaluation questions?

    Should these different groups work together on performances, or should they be separated?

    Why is it of value for these people to perform together?

    How might it be a challenge for these people to perform together?

3. Remind the YPE team that often during performances people can feel that they are being made fun of. If there is any chance of that happening between these groups, be sure to have the team separate the different groups.

4. Work with the YPE team to determine the number of performance groups and a list of people to be included. In performance, I suggest engaging between five and fifteen participants per group.

Activity: The Rehearsal

Objectives

▪ To help the YPE team members perform as directors

▪ To teach them skills to gather data using performance

Steps

1. Let the YPE team members know that to gather data through performances they will have to perfect their roles as "directors," "assistant directors," "note takers," and "observers."

2. Ask the team members if they would be willing to perform these roles with you. If they agree, create one-minute performances in which everyone plays one role (director, assistant director, note taker, or observer). Refer to Appendix B for tips on the roles of note taker and observer.

3. Once they have completed these performances, ask the following questions:

    What do we collectively know about each of these roles?

    What are the characteristics needed to perform in each role?

    What qualities do these different roles have?

   Note: If they don't come up with them on their own, you might want to review some of the following qualities:

    Directors are interested in the development of the play, stand back from the action to look at the bigger picture, help the actors try out new characteristics and explore emotions, keep the actors on track and communicating, and try new and innovative things.

    Assistant directors help the director see the bigger picture and offer the director opinions, feedback, and suggestions for redirecting the actors.

Activity: The Performance with Respondents

1. Ask the YPE team members to volunteer to perform in each of the roles (director, assistant director, note taker, and observer).

2. Make sure the note taker and the observer are ready with their performances and are working together to capture all of the information gleaned from the performances.

3. Find a room large enough to accommodate the performance activity. Be sure there is enough room to move around freely. Also, be sure that the room is private and that there are no unwanted observers.

4. Once the YPE team is ready, invite the participants into the room. Be sure to greet each one warmly so that he or she feels welcome.

5. The director (or assistant director) should read the introductory script the YPE team created regarding the purpose of the study and the use of the data.

6. The director (or assistant director) should begin the first activity in the performance script—the "icebreaker." If the group seems to have low energy, you might want to conduct two or three icebreakers to get everyone up and moving.

7. Once all the participants are on their feet and in good spirits, the directors can ask that the actors perform the specific scenes identified in the activity Creating Improvisations.

8. After each scene, discuss what happened in it with the actors and audience members (where appropriate). The following question can lead the dialogue:

   What do they think this performance was about?

   What did the characters see? Hear? Feel?

   What did they learn?

   What might they do differently if they had it to do again?

9. The director and assistant director may want to add what they saw during the performance. A play often looks different from the audience's perspective.

10. At some point during the discussion, ask the group if they would like to do the performance over again. However, this time provide actors with some new directions. For example, if one character was a bit quiet or shy, ask the actor to exaggerate his or her performance. Or if the performance was very speedy, ask the actor to do

PERFORMANCE OF A CLASSROOM Once

I was conducting an evaluation of an ESL classroom in a Brooklyn high school. The class was made up of a group of recent immigrants from twenty different countries. The teacher had been using creative improvisational activities to engage the youth in performances as "English speakers." The youth were having a terrific time and seemed to be progressing quite rapidly. Toward the end of the year I was asked to conduct a focus group with the young participants. During our discussion, they told me that this class was very different from classes in their home countries and from other classes in the school. The students weren't able to tell me exactly how the class was different, and I was having difficulty understanding their views on the subject. So I asked them if they could create performances of the classrooms and schools in their home countries. They broke into small groups to discuss their issues and create performances. Next, they staged their performances for one another. What each

---

it in slow motion. If there was a big conflict that didn't get resolved, ask the group to find a resolution during the course of the scene.

11. When the second performance is over, discuss what happened with the actors and audience members (where appropriate). Include the following questions:

What did the characters see? Hear? Feel?

How was this performance different from the last performance?

What did the participants and observers learn?

Can any of this information inform the way the YPE program operates? If so, how?

12. Continue with these playful performances until you have finished all the scenes in your script. Thank the performers for their participation, and let them know when you will be sending them a summary of the work they did.

group illustrated for me during these performances was that in their home countries, schools were much more rigid and punitive than they were in the United States. I then asked them if they would perform what it was like when they first came to their new school. Each group came back and performed. Their performances were filled with laughing, joking around, bad behavior, and a bit of chaos. After these performances, I asked the group what it was like to move from a highly structured school to one with very little structure. They told me that they felt that they weren't learning in their new school and were not being taken seriously. They missed the ways of their old schools. Next, I had them perform what it was like in this particular classroom. They gave performances of joking around and playing, but with much more structure and accountability. They told me that this class was different from others in the school because they felt the teacher did take them seriously. They were having fun, but they were also given responsibility and structure.

CHAPTER

10

USING JOURNALING IN EVALUATION

When you have finished reading this chapter, you will know more about the following:

- The definition of journal writing

- The value of journal writing as an evaluation tool

- How to work with the YPE team to create a journal protocol

- How to work with the YPE team to facilitate journal writing

- How to develop creative journal writing activities (blogs, collective journals, and so on) with the YPE team

Almost every youth program I know has used journal-writing activities to help document their practices with young people. Although journals are fantastic sources of data and often give staff greater insight into the growth of individual young people, they are rarely analyzed and therefore often useless for overall program evaluation. The use of journals and scrapbooks, along with other techniques, in monitoring your YPE team were covered in Chapter Four (see "Performing the Ensemble" in that chapter). Review that chapter as you experiment with using this creative and fun method not only with the YPE team but with other stakeholders as well.

This chapter provides helpful tips for using journal writing and scrapbooking to collect data about the program your YPE team is evaluating.

Activity: What Is Journal Writing, and How Can It Be Used as an Evaluation Tool?

Objectives

- To teach the YPE team about how journals can be used in evaluation

- To have the YPE team members brainstorm ways to use journals in their YPE project

Steps

1. Tell the members of the YPE team that they will be discussing the best ways to use journals and scrapbooks in their YPE project. Explain that the only differences between traditional journals and scrapbooks and those used in evaluation are that in evaluation we try to collect the data more systematically. In other words, when young people write in journals or add information in scrapbooks, we ask them to add very specific types of entries. Tell the team that similar to using other evaluation methods, a set of questions or issues needs to be developed to ensure that appropriate and consistent data are collected. Journals and scrapbooks can capture a wide range of data, including changes in growth, perceptions, thoughts, feelings, concerns, challenges, and successes.

2. Inform the YPE team that there are at least two types of journal writing: individual journal writing and collective journal writing. In individual journal writing, each participant is given a journal and asked to reflect on several questions or issues, recording thoughts in the journal. Collective journal writing requires that at least one member of a group or team make an entry in a collective journal every time the group meets. Journal entries can consist of prose, photographs, poetry, and drawings, among other things. Journals are generally created over long periods of time (such as a program semester or term) and should be collected and reviewed periodically by a trusted individual or group.

3. Talk to the YPE team about issues of literacy and confidentiality. Journal writing is not the best method to use with groups of young people who may have literacy challenges. It is also not the best method if you need to collect information that young people will not readily want to share.

4. Ask the YPE team members if they think either the individual or the collective method could be useful for their YPE project. Have them refer to their evaluation questions and logic models to see if this method is a good fit (see the Logic Modeling activity in Chapter Five).

Activity: Creating Journal and Scrapbook Protocols

Objectives

■ To teach the YPE team how to use journal writing to capture evaluation data

■ To help the YPE team create a journal protocol

■ To help the group develop questions that are not intimidating

■ To help the group create a structure that is easy to analyze

Steps

1. Inform the YPE team that journal writing, like interviewing and surveying, needs a type of structure or protocol.

2. Remind the YPE team members of their evaluation questions and the outcomes and indicators in their logic models. Work with them to brainstorm the types of questions they would like to ask in their journals. Possible questions include these:

   What did you do today? Please provide an example.

   How do you define social justice?

   How do you think your work is contributing to social justice?

   What did you learn today, or what new skills did you gain?

   Note: I suggest that you develop only about five questions. If there are too many, the participants won't want to write in their journals. Try to make these questions broad enough that the participants can explore their feelings and thoughts. I like to ask a combination of questions that cover participants' activities and progress for the day, their successes, and challenges they encounter. In this way, you can document their process, goals, outcomes, and other pertinent information.

Activity: Performing Journal Writing

Objective

▪ To help the YPE team perform as journal-writing facilitators

Steps

1. Let the YPE team know that there are several roles in journal writing facilitation: "journal presenter," "journal keeper," and "journal reviewer and analyst."

2. Explain to the YPE team members that the role of the journal presenter is to explain the purpose of the journal writing activities, how the data will be used, and how it will be kept confidential (if it will be kept confidential). This person must also let the respondents know whether the journals will be created individually or collectively and whether entries should be made consistently throughout a given project or over a specific period of time. Therefore, the journal presenter will need to ask the respondents to make entries in their journals either daily or weekly. Time should be set aside during the program or project to allow the participants to write in their journals.

3. Ask for volunteers to take on the responsibility of journal presenter. Ask this person or group to work together with other YPE team members to create a script to help them introduce the activity to the respondents.

4. Another major role in journal writing is that of journal keeper. This person or group reminds the participants to write in their journals and is responsible for picking them up periodically to review. Inform the YPE team that the journal keeper must keep the data absolutely confidential. Not a single person can be told what has been written in the journals. If the journal is collective, the issue of confidentiality becomes less important since everyone has agreed to make entries public.

COLLECTIVE JOURNALING The collective journal usually sat directly in the center of the table, demonstrating its importance at the very center of the youth work. This journal was very large, perhaps 17 by 24 inches. In the very beginning of the project, my colleague and I had asked for one young person to write in the journal every day. At first the group was not at all interested in this activity and did it solely because we adults said we thought it would be a good idea. At the end of every session we asked one young person to use the journal to take notes of our final reflection. Eventually, the youth began to draw in the book, take pictures of their work throughout the day and paste them in the book, draw pictures of conflicts that were happening and their end results, and document the responsibilities that people were taking and their progress toward meeting them. By the time we ended the project, the collective journal was loved by all. The young people referred to it when talking about their collective histories, and they used data in it to hold each other accountable. It was their collective institutional memory.

A staff member of an arts-based nonprofit told me of another unique example of creative journal writing. The organization's YPE team created

---

5. Tell the YPE team that in the next step, the journal reviewer and analyst will go over the data. (Chapter Eleven details how to analyze qualitative data such as these.) After the data have been analyzed, the journal reviewer and analyst will inform the members of the group of their collective accomplishments, fears, feelings, successes, challenges, and so on, during the period of time reviewed. In these "feedback sessions," it is important to highlight the similarities and differences within the group.

Note: Journal-writing data can also be used to discover individual successes and challenges. These data can then be used to help an individual participant develop his or her skills further or set higher goals. If data are going to be used in this way, be sure to let the participants know, as this often changes the tone of their writing.

Periodically, you may also want to ask for volunteers to read from their journals and share their views, thoughts, and feelings. When creating collective journals, use the journal to remind the group what activities and goals have been achieved and what challenges have arisen.

a blog on the program's Web site to document the program's ongoing process. These online journals, if you will, recorded data about how the program operated, its activities, and its outcomes. Every day, while the youth were working on their projects, one or two members from the YPE team would document their process together: take photos, create videos, write stories and poems, and draw pictures. All of this information was posted on the blog. The Web site was then advertised to the community so that everyone could monitor the young people's progress. The youth absolutely loved this process. In particular, they loved using the technology, and they were thrilled that their collective journals were public. The fact that the community actually read the journals pushed the youth to make the information accessible, interesting, and up-to-date. The blog became a serious aspect of their work that they became very proud of. Through these activities, the young people developed several new performance roles, including "blogger," "historian," "documentary artist," and "Web site developer." These performances supported the creation of multiple new ZPDs in which youth continued to grow and develop.

CHAPTER

APPROACHING DATA ANALYSIS AND REPORT WRITING CREATIVELY

When you have finished reading this chapter, you will know more about the following:

■ How to work with the YPE team to catalogue and debrief data

■ How to work with the YPE team to analyze qualitative data

■ How to work with the YPE team to analyze quantitative data

■ The components of an evaluation report

■ How to work with the YPE team to report and represent evaluation findings visually

■ How to work with the YPE team to create interactive approaches to reporting evaluation findings

At this point in your YPE project, you and your team have piles of data—thousands of words and numbers—that have been systematically collected and that describe your particular program and its outcomes for young people. Now what? This chapter provides some of the most creative and performatory strategies I have used to help a YPE team make those piles of paper smaller and produce meaning from the information in them.

The first part of the chapter covers the analysis and interpretation of data, including activities for cataloguing, debriefing, and analyzing qualitative and quantitative data. The second part of the chapter explores creative strategies for representing and sharing this information through examples of how YPE teams have presented and reported their data.

CREATIVE APPROACHES TO DATA ANALYSIS

I recommend engaging in the data analysis sessions both the full YPE team and any other stakeholders who might be interested. During these sessions I often invite various participants to review and analyze the data. I once worked with a group of youth and their board of directors to analyze the data from their YPE project that became an excellent illustration of why including different stakeholders is valuable. It turned out that the board had a very different way of understanding the data from the youth. After much debate and conversation, both received a wonderful education about each other's views and perspectives.

I can't say enough about the value of including multiple perspectives in data analysis. Youth often have very different views than adults about data, particularly data from their peers, and they understand subtle subtexts that adults will never catch because of their distance from the youth culture.

Qualitative data include words, sentences, stories, pictures, drawings, and maps. Qualitative data generally come from surveys, interviews, focus groups, journals, and other sources. Quantitative data are numbers, such as the number of young people in the program, the number of activities, the number of responses to a survey question, grades, and test scores. Quantitative data are generally collected through surveys, tests, rating activities, and other instruments.

Activity: Cataloguing and Debriefing Qualitative Data

Objectives

- To help the YPE team manage data throughout the data collection process

■ To ensure that data are properly catalogued and sorted prior to analysis

Steps

1. Let the members of the YPE team know that they should set aside time after every data collection strategy (interviewing, focus groups, surveys) to review their notes and make sure they have captured all the information clearly. The notes should be neat enough that anyone can read them, and responses should be located under the corresponding questions. Making sure the data are neat and in good order makes the analysis process much easier.

2. After each data collection method, members of the YPE team should check the demographic data sheets to make sure they have captured all the information they need. (This should be done before the respondents leave the room in order to follow up on missing data.) These data sheets should be placed in a folder and labeled, including the date (for example, "Demographic Information from Interviews Conducted with Youth Media Team, May 20, 2008").

3. If the YPE team has taped the interviews, make sure the tapes are properly marked and stored in a folder or envelope. These tapes should be kept with your interview responses and debriefing notes in a secure and confidential location.

4. After each data collection method, the YPE team should meet to debrief. Ask everyone to break into small teams—this activity should be done in small teams because most of the data was collected in teams. Have each team read through the data. Specifically, have team members look for any information that "stands out," in their opinion. Ask them to record their general responses to the data—for example, What do they think is being said? Is it positive or negative? Also, ask them to record any patterns or themes that emerge from the data: issues, words, responses that keep cropping up. This debriefing is the first level of data analysis, and the YPE team members will use these notes later in their qualitative and quantitative analyses.

5. Once they have finished reading and taking notes, discuss the following questions:

How did the method go? Did the respondents understand what you were asking them to do? Why or why not?

Were the respondents able to complete the method, or were there challenges? In other words, were they able to answer all of the questions in the interview protocol or focus group or on the survey? What questions did respondents get stuck on?

What are some of your first impressions about the data? (For example, were they positive, negative, thoughtful, not thoughtful?)

What kinds of points arose more than once in the data?

What surprised you most? Why?

What responses didn't surprise you at all? Why?

What did you learn?

Note: Be sure to have one of the YPE team members take notes throughout the debriefing.

Activity: Qualitative Data Analysis

Objectives

■ To introduce the YPE team to qualitative program analysis

■ To help the YPE team recognize patterns or themes in the collected data

■ To help the YPE team create codes for these patterns or themes

■ To help the YPE team interpret the findings

Steps

1. Once all of the data have been catalogued and all of the answers are under the corresponding questions, you can begin your analysis process.

2. Let the members of the YPE team know that they should start by looking at the demographic data sheets. Ask them to review these sheets and write summary statements about the types of respondents in your sample—for example, "20 youth were interviewed.

Of these, most ($n = 15$) were 15 years of age, a few ($n = 4$) were 13 years of age, and 1 was 9 years of age."

3. Once these demographic summary statements are complete, ask the YPE team to think about the group of respondents. Does the team want to look at the data collected from this group as a whole? Or are there other ways in which the team would like to sort the data? For example, do team members want to look at gender differences? Differences based on length of time in the program? Differences between young people who participated in different activities or groups?

   Note: These types of differences are generally easier to examine in interview data.

4. Next, copy all of the qualitative data (interviews, stories, or focus group notes) so that you are not working with the originals. If the YPE team is interested in examining differences in an interview group—gender, for example—consider copying the interviews on different-colored paper (yellow for the girls and green for the boys, perhaps) so that the differences are visual.

5. Next, cut each of the questions and responses out of the protocols and put them together on one piece of paper or all in one place. When working with interview data, there will be stacks of questions and responses for question 1, question 2, and so on. Put these data in separate envelopes. For example, all responses to question 1 will go in one envelope marked "Question 1." When working with focus group data, the YPE team should create a separate response sheet for each question. Each sheet should contain the question and all of the responses.

6. Ask the YPE team to break up into small teams. Each team can be responsible for analyzing and interpreting a small set of questions. Hand out the envelopes or response sheets. Also hand out copies of the debriefing notes (or post the flipchart page) to remind the team members of their initial impressions about the data.

7. Working with one question at a time, the teams should lay out all of the data on a table or post the data on a wall and then read through the responses. Tell them they are looking for patterns or themes that emerge as they read. For example, the following statements were made by youth about their program: "It made me think in a new and creative ways"; "I began to think differently"; "It

changed my thinking to see things I wouldn't have seen." This is a pattern, and the YPE team termed it "thinking outside the box." Every time team members saw this kind of statement in the data, they made a note in the margin with the code or symbol they assigned to "thinking outside the box."

8. Ask the following questions to help the teams analyze and interpret their data:

> What are some of your first impressions about the data? (Were they positive, negative, thoughtful, not thoughtful?)
>
> What points arose more than once in the data? What themes or patterns are emerging?
>
> How many of the responses are the same or similar?
>
> Were there any differences in the data that could be attributed to a specific group (based on gender, ethnicity, length of time in the program, participation in certain activities, and so on)?
>
> How do these patterns relate to the overall evaluation question?
>
> Are there any deviations from any of the patterns? If yes, what kinds? How many of the responses are different? Are there any factors that might help explain these deviations (gender of the respondent, the length of time in the program, and so on)?
>
> Are there any surprises? What are these?
>
> What responses didn't surprise you at all? Why?
>
> Are there any interesting quotes that can be used or stories that further explain or exemplify a particular pattern? Can these stories or examples be used to help illuminate the broader evaluation question?
>
> Do these patterns match other findings that you have discovered while collecting other types of data for the evaluation? If not, what might explain these differences?

9. When the teams have finished, they can come together to compare and contrast their analyses. During this sharing process, the YPE team can begin to see if there are any trends across the questions. Have each team present its responses to each of the questions. Starting with the first question, have the team share its responses, examining

collective answers and exploring similarities and differences. Take notes on a flipchart. Be sure to note any differences across groups, such as those based on gender, ethnicity, race, class, group type, or length of time in the program.

10. Once the codes and patterns have been identified, have the YPE team go back through the interviews to see the extent to which a pattern code applies. For example, if the YPE team has identified "thinking outside the box" as a pattern, then members would need to go back through all of the data to determine the number of respondents who talked about "thinking outside the box" or "thinking in a different and creative way."

11. Work with the YPE team to create summary statements of the data. In analyzing interviews, for example, the team can create a summary statement about each question on the interview like this one:

> All of the youth interviewed stated that the program had had a positive impact on their lives. Almost all (22 of the 25) youth interviewed stated that they learned how to speak out about issues that were important to them and had gained leadership skills. For example, one youth made the following statement: "I learned how to stand up for myself and speak up when I need to. I have been doing this in class all year, and other students admire me for that. They now see me as a leader."

You can also make broader summary statements about the data, for example:

> All of the adults and youth stated that the program was valuable to youth. In particular, all stated that youth "learned new skills," "learned to work in groups," "learned how to respect one another," "developed positive relationships with adults." However, one or two parents stated that the program did not do a good job of "supporting academic success."

Quantitative Data Analysis

Quantitative data analysis can be extremely complicated. In my experience with YPE projects, however, teams usually need only a basic tally of responses from their surveys. Analyzing the data is as simple as counting the frequency of responses. In some instances I have worked with YPE teams to hand-count their responses, and in others I have helped them set up spreadsheets. Luckily, in almost every YPE team at least one young person falls in love with data entry and data analysis. Generally, it takes only a few minutes to teach a young person how to do this type of work.

Unfortunately, within the scope of this chapter, it is not possible for me to write out an exact strategy for training a young person to set up a database. However, if you can find the money, I recommend training a few youth to enter and analyze qualitative data—it will be one of the best investments you make. If you find the right youth, they will be fantastic at the task and love doing it. And they will gain a valuable new skill at the same time.

It always surprises me which young people end up loving quantitative data analysis. In many cases, these same youth told me adamantly that they hated numbers and could not operate a computer. However, once they see how simple data entry and analysis are, many young people quickly get the hang of it, and it becomes a pleasure. Many years ago I worked with a young woman who made it clear to me that she would not participate in data entry or analysis. So the YPE team began working with one of the boys. After he dropped the job, the task fell to her, and she was not at all sure she could handle it. I asked for her impression of a data analyst. She said they were boring nerds who were very smart—not like her at all. I told her that it might be boring, but I knew she was smart enough to perform the task. I also assured her that she probably would not turn into a nerd. But I cautioned, "Who knows? Anything can happen!" That was over seven years ago, and she has turned into one of the best data analysts I know. She still calls me to talk about her program's database.

Activity: Hand-Tallying and Setting Up a Database

Objectives

- To help the YPE team analyze qualitative data
- To teach the YPE team how to summarize data

Steps

1. Number all of the surveys. Numbering serves two purposes: if you lose one, you will know, and if you have any questions about the data, you can go back to a specific survey.

2. Make a copy of a blank survey to use as a template to record responses.

3. Starting with question 1, count the number of times people responded to each of the response categories, and mark it on the blank survey template. For example, if the first question on the survey was "How long have you participated in this program?" and the response options were "under six months," "seven months to one year," "one year to two years," and "more than two years," you would need to record the number of people who marked each of these responses. For example, 5 youth had participated for "under six months," 80 had participated for "seven months to one year," 120 had participated for "one year to two years," and none had participated for longer. Explain to the YPE team that this activity is called an analysis of "frequency": you are counting the frequency of occurrence of each particular response.

4. Once you have summarized all of the data on the survey in this manner, you may need to do a cross-tabulation, or "cross-tab." A cross-tab is a way of sorting the data to see differences in responses by gender, ethnicity, length of time in the program, and so on. If you want to do a cross-tab by gender, you can create three sets of data: one for the males, one for the females, and one for transgender youth. This time start with three blank surveys. Be sure to title each "Males," "Females," or "Transgender." Next, go through the same process in Step 3 and recount the data. When you have finished all three sets, check the figures to see if they add up to the total that was noted on the overall survey analysis template.

Note: When working with data in this way, make several copies of the data so that the YPE team can break up into smaller teams and work on different questions at the same time. This is an effective strategy, particularly if the survey is long and involved. (If there are open-ended questions on the survey, refer to the discussion of qualitative analysis earlier in this chapter.)

Also, you can have the YPE team take whole numbers and turn them into percentages. One word of caution: do not create percentages with very small populations, as this often distorts the findings. The rule of thumb is to use percentages only when you have a total population of one hundred or more. However, in small program evaluations there are often fewer than one hundred youth. In these situations, percentages can be useful for comparisons. But be sure to report the exact population at the same time. The population is often presented in parentheses, preceded by a lowercase n, which stands for "number." For example, "Most of the youth (95%, $n = 45$) stated that the program was beneficial to them; 55% ($n = 26$) reported that it helped them learn new skills." The total number of respondents (in other words, 100 percent of the population), is represented by a capital N.

5. Have the YPE team develop summary statements of the data; for example:

> Almost all of the youth (85%, $n = 75$) stated that the program helped them develop new skills. In particular, most young people (95%, $n = 84$) reported learning how to use new technology, more than half (65%, $n = 57$) reported learning how to conduct presentations, and some (35%, $n = 31$) reported learning how to create a Web site.

CREATIVE STRATEGIES FOR PRESENTING DATA

Evaluation reports can be extremely helpful to key stakeholders, but for that to happen we all must get better at presenting our findings in ways that are useful to the programs. For some reason, although there are many creative strategies for presenting and sharing data, very few evaluators use them. Instead, we (I must include myself) insist on writing long, boring reports and PowerPoint presentations. On the other hand, young people are enormously imaginative when it comes to putting together presentations on their YPE projects. They use videos, performance, scrapbooks, "did you know?" memos, talk show formats, posters, and photos. My suggestion is to let youth take the creative lead in this process.

In this part of the chapter I will describe some interesting examples of evaluation presentations that youth and program staff have created, grouped into two categories, visual representations and interactive presentations.

Before getting to the examples, I suggest looking over the following sample evaluation report outline. No matter which creative format your team uses, a YPE report should include the following components.

Typical YPE Report Outline

I. Introduction to your program

   A. What is the focus of your program?

    B. Who are your participants?

    C. What critical strategies does your program use?

II. Purpose of your YPE project

    A. What are the general issues you are exploring?

    B. Why are these issues important to the YPE team and the program?

    C. Who is affected or most invested in these issues?

    D. What is interesting or provocative about these issues, and why do they have meaning or relevance for people in your program?

III. YPE questions

    A. What are your YPE questions?

    B. What types of data did you collect to answer these questions?

IV. Data collection methods

    A. Which methods did you use, and which questions did they help answer?

    B. Why did you choose these methods?

    C. How often were these methods used?

    D. Who were your respondents? How many were there? Why were these individuals chosen? What is their relationship to the total population?

    E. Why did you choose this group of respondents?

    F. Who conducted the data collection?

    G. Were your methods confidential or anonymous?

V. Data analysis and interpretation

    A. How and when were the data analyzed and interpreted?

    B. Who participated in the analysis?

    C. How often did you meet to review the data?

VI. YPE findings

    A. What were the key findings from the data?

B. After grouping the findings under the evaluation questions, were all questions answered by the data?

C. Do all the data in the report help answer the evaluation questions?

D. Are the findings reported exactly as the data illustrate? (It is important not to interpret the data, explain them, or draw any conclusions at this point.)

VII. YPE conclusions and recommendations

A. What conclusions have you drawn from the data?

B. What do these data and these conclusions mean to the YPE team?

C. What are your recommendations for the program? Have any of your recommendations already been implemented? If so, which ones?

Before you begin thinking about the type of report you would like to create, remember that no matter how you represent the YPE data—visually, in written form, or interactively—try to share information frequently so that all stakeholders are informed throughout the process. Think about holding multiple forums and meetings to allow stakeholders to engage in an ongoing conversation about the findings and their implications for the program. Don't wait until the last minute. The idea is to make midcourse corrections throughout the process.

Visual Representations of Data

On the Road. One program I had been working with for years decided that all of its work with young people revolved around three basic outcomes: caring, ability, and respect. These became affectionately known throughout the program as CAR. The staff were committed to participatory evaluation processes and wanted to make sure that youth, parents, and staff all understood how the program was doing in its efforts toward obtaining these outcomes. In the front lobby of the program's office, the staff erected a giant two-dimensional car and a construction paper road that wound its way through the hallways. The road represented the evaluation timeline, and all along it youth posted various projects and samples of their work. There were six "refueling stations" along the road, representing the six different semesters when data were collected. Once an analysis was completed, all the information was posted at the refueling station for everyone to see. A giant gas station stood at the end of the road, with an analysis of the entire year's data. Parents and youth loved to visit the road and see how the program was doing; they could look to see the results of the parent survey or how the third graders felt the staff were doing in terms of their caring, ability, and respect.

Did You Know? I have also worked with youth to write "did you know?" memos. These memos are sent to key stakeholders after every data collection. In this way, everyone is informed about evaluation results throughout the process and can read the results in small, manageable increments. Often these memos are presented during staff and youth team meetings so that everyone can review and discuss the results.

Multimedia. In other programs, youth and staff have created videos showing excerpts from interviews and footage of their process as a YPE team. Several groups I have worked with have used photos (both print and slide shows), picture storyboards, and poster displays of their evaluation process and findings. A recent YPE team I have worked with set up a Web page on MySpace.com, where the team members posted their entire YPE process and all of their findings. Connected to this page was a blog where other young people could discuss the results of the YPE team evaluation.

Interactive Representation of Data

The Game Show. One of my favorite interactive formats for sharing evaluation data is the game show format. For example, I might ask a group of stakeholders to try to guess the responses to various questions on a survey or an interview. I generally enlarge the questions and "correct responses" on flipchart pages and cover the "correct responses" with paper or Post-it notes. I ask the audience, "How do you think the youth responded to the following question?" After people have shouted out their answers, I reveal the "correct response." I have also done this game by creating teams that play against each other to guess the most correct responses. The game is successful as an evaluation tool because everyone gets very involved in trying to determine the right answer, and there are many debates about why they got it right or wrong.

The Play's the Thing. Not surprisingly, another very successful interactive strategy for presenting YPE reports is performance. A number of times I have worked with a team to write a script of its YPE report and then perform it. Usually, a YPE team breaks into small groups to work on different aspects of the script, using the components of the YPE report outline as a guide, and then to create performances to represent their YPE process and methods as well as their findings. This is a particularly good strategy when there are a lot of qualitative data, as some youth can perform the views of a particular set of respondents or constituents and others can perform a different set of views and beliefs. Direct quotes from the data can be used too as part of the script. At the end of these performances, we generally conduct discussions, asking members of the audience about their interpretation of the key evaluation findings and any recommendations they might have for the program. These conversations are usually very revealing and elicit extremely creative recommendations. I suggest documenting these discussions so that they can be used for further planning. This can be done by videotaping, taking notes, or photographing the session.

CHAPTER

ENCOURAGEMENTS

When you have finished reading this chapter, you will be eager to conduct your own YPE projects and be careful to do all of the following things:

- Continuously create the ensemble and the performatory environment
- Keep working on your performance as director
- Treat youth as who they are becoming
- Help youth and yourself perform in advance of yourselves
- Build with everything you have

This book has been a joy to write. I have loved remembering the work I have done over the years with so many wonderful young people from around the world. Through writing about my experiences, I have been able to polish them and make them more accessible. Of course, only my successes have been documented, and this one-sided picture is the problem with most books. The end product erases the messy production process. It is as if the often chaotic activity of creation does not exist, and books fall from the heavens, perfectly packaged with all the right answers. As readers, we are not privy to the "real" process. In my case that includes the many activities I tried over the years that bombed, my struggle to present years of work with youth in a coherent and interesting way, the missed deadlines, the seemingly endless revisions, and the many people who provided ideas and suggestions throughout the writing of this book.

The finished product can make it seem as if the person writing the book (me, in this case) knows much more than the reader (you, in this case). To top it off, as the reader you are now being asked to replicate my work in your own program—by yourself, with little support except for this book. The reason I am inviting you to go through this difficult process is because it has been a completely transformative and joyful experience for me and I believe it really works. But don't take my word for it; try one of the activities and see. Just pick one that sounds like the most fun and try it out. I think that you too will have an amazing experience. I also want to encourage you to play with the methodologies and activities I have laid out and to create your own, moving beyond my work to build the field. If this book is about anything, it is about creative collaborative activity; it is about trying new things, taking big creative risks, and not knowing.

One creative risk that you will encounter in doing YPE will be talking about your work. People will not always get it. This type of performatory work with youth requires a paradigm shift, moving away from individualism and particulars toward totalities. Given that our cultural assumptions and practices are geared to the individual, staying focused on the development of the group rather than on the development of the group members can be very challenging. And it is even harder to take the posture of not knowing in a world that so values knowing.

There is something beyond cognitive learning that happens during performance, and this is very difficult to describe. For example, I was once asked to participate in a conference in Mexico on the subject of promising practices for engaging young people in knowledge production. About thirty adult participants were there, almost all of them academics. Most of these educators and theorists were very concerned that the young researchers' thoughts, feelings, views, and emotions might be completely corrupted by the adults if they weren't careful. Both I and another person, both of us theater artists, kept trying to introduce the notion of ensemble creation, in which all members of the group take responsibility for the production and learn and grow together. We talked to the group about the benefits of engaging in this type of activity, and it seemed that everyone was in agreement. However, the group immediately went back to the discussion about youth versus adults and valid versus invalid data collection strategies.

At some point, my theatrical colleague got frustrated and said, "I see that everyone is talking about 'relevant knowledge production.' Kim and I are talking about 'irrelevant knowledge production.'" This quote, and my new friend, have stuck with me. I love thinking about my work in terms of its irrelevance. He was right: most people see performance and collective activity as irrelevant knowledge. And this group was no different. It is understandable why these people didn't "get it"—they simply did not have a framework for what we were talking about.

It has been my experience that the people who get it are those who have experienced some type of performance or creative ensemble work. These folks intuitively know that something about them has been qualitatively transformed through these processes. As a society we have very little language to describe these types of experiences, yet we all know they are extremely powerful. People often say that these experiences seem "bigger than me" or "larger than life." Perhaps this is because they are larger than any one individual's experience—they are collective experiences.

It is difficult to find the appropriate language to describe creative ensemble work. The language we have just does not represent the totality of the experience. It is not only verbal; it is physical, emotional, social, playful, and participatory. All of this cannot be described with mere words. It must be experienced.

So I want to encourage you to keep creating environments in which people can experience performance and creative play. I will close by leaving you with a few tips for how to maintain your performatory posture.

FIVE TIPS FOR MAINTAINING YOUR PERFORMATORY POSTURE

1. *Continuously create the ensemble and the performatory environment*. Remember to keep your focus on the ongoing creation of the ensemble. See and relate to everything as performance, or as one possible way of being in the world. In this way, roles can be changed, redefined, exaggerated, and otherwise manipulated. Let the members of the group know that they (and you) are all responsible for building and creating an environment in which everyone can grow and develop.

2. *Keep working on your performance as director*. Sometimes a director will say to an actor, "Why did you make that choice?" or "That choice didn't work; try this one." It is not a moral statement. Some choices simply do not work for the play. A director needs to help the actors see how their actions contribute to the overall play. How liberating

it would be if we all had directors in our lives who could tell us when our performances were good choices and when they were not working so well!

We humans move in and out of so many different plays throughout a given week or day that it is difficult to keep up. In fact, we often do not even recognize that we have moved from one play into the next. Consequently, we struggle to "catch up" or "catch on" to our new roles. Somehow, most of us manage. But as you develop your role as director, you will become acutely aware of this shift in play. You may also find that as you become more aware of these various plays, you develop a stronger performance for each.

Be sure to invite young people to perform as directors along with you. Invite them to relate to your work together as one possible play that can be directed and redirected creatively. Through the ensemble work, most members of the YPE team will learn how to direct the various plays and performances the group performs. Encourage all YPE team members to become responsible for not only participating in the performances but also for directing them. In this way they willingly take on the hard work of continuously improving the performance of the group.

3. *Treat youth as who they are becoming.* One aspect of building a creative ensemble is treating all members of the team as who they are becoming, or as Lev Vygotsky says, "as a head taller." I recently watched an episode of *The Dog Whisperer* and realized how much of his philosophy mirrored my own. In particular, he was working with a young woman who had a very difficult dog. This dog would not come out from under the woman's desk; he was completely antisocial. No matter how hard the woman pulled, pushed, and prodded, he just wouldn't budge. But when the dog whisperer took hold of the leash, the dog immediately came out. The woman was shocked. The dog whisperer explained that the dog responded to him because he believed that the dog would do it. He related to the dog as capable of coming out from under the desk. In his estimation, this woman not only needed to believe that the dog would come out from under the desk but also needed to move her body in such a way that the dog knew she believed it. He explained that the dog could actually read her energy and "knew" that she didn't think he could do it. She made several attempts and was finally able to change her attitude and her body language—her performance. The dog came out from under the desk and became a social animal.

Like all animals, humans can "read" how others feel about them or how others see them. Whether we like it or not, these views affect our performances. It is important, then, when we work with groups, to create developmental performance environments where we encourage everyone to relate to everyone else as "who they are becoming."

4. *Help youth and yourself perform "in advance of yourselves."* It is important that we learn how to do things we do not yet know how to do, so be sure to provide multiple opportunities for everyone in the group to perform "in advance of themselves." Performance allows us to try on roles, skill sets, emotions, and views before we actually know what we are doing. It is through the activity of performing what we do not know that we develop.

5. *Build with everything you have.* Don't get trapped in the belief that as the adult you have to structure everything for the young people. Continue to draw on their knowledge and lack of knowledge, their experiences and lack of experiences, and their emotions, positive and negative. Build with their friendships and their conflicts with one another. In your new performance as director, everything can be seen as fantastic material for the ongoing development of the play.

CONCLUDING THOUGHT

After a couple of hundred pages, I hope I have finally explained what it is I do for a living! Now I need to go back to my hometown and do a little performance work—the next family holiday is just around the corner.

APPENDIX

TIPS FOR THE INTERVIEWER

Step 1

■ Introduce yourself to the respondent or respondents, and provide the following information:

> Explain why you want to interview them. Let them know that the primary purpose of the interview is to achieve a clear understanding of their perspectives about a particular issue or about the program and its impact.

> Let them know how long the interview will take (often an hour or less; never plan on taking more than two hours).

> Give an overview of the YPE project and how the interview fits into the overall evaluation process.

Step 2

■ If you intend to tape the conversation, ask the permission of the respondents before you turn on the tape recorder. Explain that there

This appendix is adapted from material created with Catlin Fullwood for the Cricket Island Foundation.

will also be someone taking notes so that you can concentrate on the questions and responses. Introduce the note taker to the respondents.

■ Explain that the notes will capture the primary points that come up and that some quotes may be used in the report. Stress that no names or identifying information will be used.

Step 3

■ Start the tape recorder (if you are taping the interview).

■ Use the questions agreed on by the YPE team. Use probes (follow-up questions for clarification) when appropriate.

■ Make sure each question is fully answered. Do not allow a respondent to go too far off track. This is your only chance to hear from people in this kind of setting, so you want to go as deep as possible *and* cover all the questions. Be mindful of the time, and move through the questions accordingly.

■ Make clear transitions from one section of the interview protocol to the next so that respondents understand the connection between questions.

■ Make sure that the note taker is doing the job appropriately and is able to keep up with the pace of the interview. You might politely ask a respondent to slow down if necessary to capture particularly interesting quotes.

Step 4

■ Let respondents know when you have reached the last question, and ask if there is anything more they would like to add.

■ Thank the respondents for their participation and their thoughtful wisdom.

■ Explain the next steps of the process and what will happen with the information.

■ Hold a debriefing session with the note taker immediately after the interviewer. Compare your impressions. Discuss and clarify the notes, and have the note taker write them up in as much detail as possible.

TIPS FOR THE NOTE TAKER

- Help put respondents at ease by chatting with them and letting them know you are glad they are participating.

- Be knowledgeable about the overall process so that you can answer questions that are addressed to you. If you do not know an answer, find it.

- Do not try to capture everything the respondents say; record only the main points. Ask the interviewer to stop for a moment if there is a good quote that you would like to write down verbatim.

- Follow the format of the questions for your notes, and jot down key points that the respondent makes in response to each.

- Be sure to note when an issue or theme is repeated.

- Keep an eye on the tape recorder to make sure it is working. If it stops, gently ask the interviewer to pause. Be sure to label the tape immediately: side one and side two, with the name and date of the interview on both sides.

- Meet with the interviewer to debrief the interview as soon as it is over. Write up your notes. Use the tapes to reference points you may have missed and to double-check your impressions and quotations.

APPENDIX

TIPS FOR CONDUCTING FOCUS GROUPS

Materials Needed

- Notepads and pens for the facilitator
- Flipchart, markers, and tape for the note taker
- Food
- Name tags for all participants
- A set of questions for the facilitator and the note taker
- Consent forms for the participants
- Demographic data sheets for participants
- Ten to fifteen participants

This appendix is adapted from material created with Catlin Fullwood for the Cricket Island Foundation.

TIPS FOR THE FACILITATOR

Step 1

■ Introduce yourself to participants as they arrive, and give them a name tag, explaining that they should use only their first names.

■ Make people feel welcome when they arrive, particularly if they don't know one another.

■ Distribute demographic data sheets or other survey instruments for people to fill out while the group is gathering.

Step 2

■ It is preferable to have respondents sit in a circle so that everyone can see everyone else.

■ Explain that the purpose of the focus group is to hear what the participants think on a particular issue. Give an overview of the YPE project, and explain how the focus group fits into the overall evaluation process. Discuss confidentiality and explain the release forms you are asking people to sign.

■ Introduce the observer and explain that he or she will not participate but will observe the process and take notes. Explain that the notes will capture the primary points that come up and that some quotes may be used in the report. Stress that no names or identifying information will be used.

Step 3

■ Use the questions agreed on with the YPE team. Use probes (follow-up questions for clarification) when appropriate.

■ Make sure each question is fully answered. Do not allow a respondent to go too far off track. This is your only chance to hear from people in this kind of setting, so you want to go as deep as possible *and* cover all the questions. Be mindful of the time, and move through the questions accordingly. (You do not want the session to last more than two hours.)

■ Make clear transitions from one section of the focus group protocol to the next so that the group understands the connection between questions.

■ Make sure the note taker is doing the job appropriately and is able to keep up with the group.

Step 4

■ Let the group know when you have reached the last question.

■ Thank all participants for their participation and their thoughtful wisdom.

■ Explain the next steps of the process and what will happen with the information.

■ Acknowledge that this process might bring up some hard issues for people and that you will be available at the end of the session if anyone wants to talk further about issues that were raised.

TIPS FOR THE NOTE TAKER

■ Distribute the demographic sheets, and make sure everyone understands how to fill it out.

■ Help put people at ease by chatting with them and letting them know you are glad they are participating.

■ Be knowledgeable about the overall process so that you can answer questions that are addressed to you. If you do not know an answer, find it.

■ Do not try to capture everything the participants say; record only the main points.

■ Follow the format of the question protocol for your notes, and jot down key points that people make under each.

■ You are looking for themes, so be sure to note when something is repeated or said several times but in different ways.

■ Record interesting quotes, but do not use names in your notes.

APPENDIX

HOW TO DETERMINE THE APPROPRIATE SAMPLE SIZE

As shown in Table C.1, when a sample is comparatively large, adding cases provides little additional precision.

As population size increases, the total size of the sample becomes proportionately smaller without affecting error.

When the population size is small, relatively large proportions are required to produce reasonable error rates.

A standard proportion will not work as a sampling strategy for varying population sizes.

Rule of thumb: you must always draw a larger sample than what is planned.

Source: Baker & Sabo (2004), appendix.

TABLE C.1. Sample Size Needed at the 95% Confidence
Level for Various Degrees of Precision.

	SAMPLING ERROR		
Population Size (*N*)	±3%	±5%	±10%
100	92	80	49
250	203	152	70
500	341	217	81
750	441	254	85
1,000	516	278	88
2,500	748	333	93
5,000	880	357	94
10,000	964	370	95
25,000	1,023	378	96
50,000	1,045	381	96
100,000	1,056	383	96
1,000,000	1,066	384	96
100,000,000	1,067	384	96

Adapted from Reisman (2000).

REFERENCES

Baker, A., & Sabo, K. (2004). *Participatory evaluation essentials: A guide for funders and their non-profit organizations and evaluation partners.* Cambridge, MA: Bruner Foundation.

Calvert, M., Zeldin, S., & Weisenbach, A. (2002). *Youth involvement for community, organizational and youth development: Directions for research, evaluation, and practice.* Madison: University of Wisconsin-Madison & Innovation Center for Community and Youth Development/Tides Center.

Camino, L. (1992). *What differences do racial, ethnic, and cultural differences make in youth development programs?* Washington, DC: Carnegie Council on Adolescent Development.

Camino, L. (2001). *Evaluation as a tool in community building: Perspectives on the role of youth.* Paper presented at the annual meeting of the American Evaluation Association, Saint Louis.

Camino, L. (2005). Pitfalls and promising practices of youth-adult partnerships: An evaluator's reflections. *Journal of Community Psychology, 33*(1), 75–85.

Camino, L., & Zeldin, S. (1999). Youth leadership: Linking research and program theory to exemplary practice. *New Designs for Youth Development, 15*(1), 10–15.

Checkoway, B., & Finn, J. (1992). *Young people as community builders.* Ann Arbor: University of Michigan School of Social Work.

Checkoway, B., Dobbie, E., & Richards-Schuster, K. (2003). The Wingspread Symposium: Involving young people in community evaluation research. *CYD Journal, 4*(1), 7–11.

Cousins, J. B., Donohue, J. J., & Bloom, G. A. (1996). Collaborative evaluation in North America: Evaluators' self-reported opinions, practices, and consequences. *Evaluation Practice, 17*(3), 207–226.

Cousins, J. B., & Whitmore, E. (1998). Framing participatory evaluation. In E. Whitmore (Ed.), *Understanding and practicing participatory evaluation.* New Directions for Evaluation, Vol. 80. San Francisco: Jossey-Bass.

Fetterman, D. M., Kaftarian, S. J., & Wandersman, A. (Eds.). (1996). *Empowerment evaluation: Knowledge and tools for self-assessment and accountability.* Thousand Oaks, CA: Sage.

Ginwright, S., & James, T. (2002). From assets to agents of change: Social justice, organizing, and youth development. In R. D. Macy, S. Barry, & G. G. Noam (Eds.), *Youth facing threat and terror: Supporting preparedness and resilience.* New Directions for Youth Development, Vol. 96. San Francisco: Jossey-Bass.

Golombek, S. (2002). *What works in youth participation: Case studies from around the world.* Baltimore: International Youth Foundation.

Hart, R. (1997). *Children's participation: The theory and practice of involving young citizens in community development and environmental care.* London: EarthScan.

Heath, S. B. (2000). Making learning work. *Afterschool Matters, 1*(1), 33–45.

Holzman, L. (1995). Creating developmental learning environments: A Vygotskian practice. *School Psychology International, 16*(2), 199–212.

Holzman, L. (1997). *Schools for growth: Radical alternatives to current educational models.* Mahwah, NJ: Erlbaum.

Holzman, L. (2004, May). *What is the "social" in "social development"?* Paper presented at the Social Development, Social Inequalities and Social Justice Conference of the Jean Piaget Society, Toronto.

Horsch, K., Little, P. M. D., Chase Smith, J., Goodyear, L., & Harris, E. (2002). Youth involvement in evaluation and research: Issues and opportunities. *Out-of-School Time Evaluation Briefs, 1.*

James, T. (1997). Empowerment through social change. *Fridges, 3*(4), 6–7.

James, T. (2001). The media: A tool for change? *Evaluation Exchange, 7*(1).

James, T., & McGillicuddy, K. (2001). Building youth movements for community change. *Nonprofit Quarterly, 8*(4), 1–3.

Kirshner, B., O'Donoghue, J. L., & McLaughlin, M. W. (2002). *Youth community engagement: A sociocultural study of participatory action research.* Stanford, CA: Stanford University, John W. Gardner Center for Youth and Their Communities.

Larson, R., Jarrett, R., Hansen, D., Pearce, N., Sullivan, P., Walker, K., Watkins, N., & Wood, D. (2003). Organized youth activities as contexts for positive development. In P. A. Linley & S. Joseph (Eds.), *Positive psychology in practice* (pp. 540–560). New York: Wiley.

Lewis-Charp, H., Yu, H. C., & Soukamneuth, S. (2006). Civic activist approaches for engaging youth in social justice. In S. Ginwright, P. Noguera, & J. Cammarota (Eds.), *Beyond resistance! Youth activism and community change* (pp. 21–36). New York: Routledge.

London, J. (2000). *Youth-led research, evaluation, and planning. The experience of youth in focus.* Las Vegas, NV: Focal Point.

London, J., O'Connor, C., and Camino, L. (2005). *Step by step: An introduction to youth-led evaluation and research.* Youth in Focus.

London, J., Zimmerman, K., & Erbstein, N. (2003). Youth-led research, evaluation and planning as youth, organizational and community development. In K. Sabo-Flores (Ed.), Youth participatory evaluation: A field in the making. New Directions in Evaluation, Vol. 98. San Francisco: Jossey-Bass.

Newman, F., & Holzman, L. (1993). *Lev Vygotsky: Revolutionary scientist.* London: Routledge.

Newman, F., & Holzman, L. (1996). *Unscientific psychology: A cultural-performatory approach to understanding human life.* Westport, CT: Praeger.

Patton, M. Q. (1997). *Utilization-focused evaluation: The new century text* (3rd ed.). Thousand Oaks, CA: Sage.

Pittman, K., & Wright, M. (1991). *Bridging the gap: A rationale for enhancing the role of community organizations in promoting youth development.* Washington, DC: Academy for Educational Development.

Reisman, J. (2000). *A field guide to outcome-based program evaluation.* Seattle, WA: Evaluation Forum.

Sabo, K. (1999). *Young people's involvement in evaluating the programs that serve them.* Dissertation, City University of New York, Graduate School.

Sabo, K. (2003a). Editor's note. In K. Sabo-Flores (Ed.), *Youth participatory evaluation: A field in the making.* New Directions in Evaluation, Vol. 98. San Francisco: Jossey-Bass.

Sabo, K. (Ed.). (2003b). A Vygotskian perspective on youth participatory evaluation. In K. Sabo-Flores (Ed.), *Youth participatory evaluation: A field in the making*. New Directions in Evaluation, Vol. 98. San Francisco: Jossey-Bass.

Senge, P. (1990). *The fifth discipline*. New York: Doubleday.

Sherrod, L. R., Flanagan, C., & Youniss, J. (2002). Dimensions of citizenship and opportunities for youth development: The what, why, when, where, and who of citizenship development. *Applied Developmental Science, 6*(4), 264–272.

Sommers M. (2001). *Care and protection of children in emergencies: A field guide*. Westport, CT: Save the Children.

Vygotsky, L .S. (1978). *Mind in society*. Cambridge, MA: Harvard University Press.

Wheeler, W. (2000). Emerging organizational theory and the youth development. *Applied Developmental Science, 4*(1), 47–54.

Youniss, J., Bales, S., Christmas-Best, V., Diversis, M., McLaughlin, M., and Silbereisen, R. (2002). Youth civic engagement in the twenty-first century. *Journal of Research on Adolescence, 12*, 121–148.

Youth in Focus. (2002). *Youth REP step by step: An introduction to youth-led research and evaluation*. Oakland, CA: Youth in Focus.

Zeldin, S. (2004). Youth as agents of adult and community development: Mapping the process and outcomes of youth engaged in organizational governance. *Applied Developmental Science, 8*(2), 75–90.

Zeldin, S., Larson, R., Camino, L., & O'Connor, C. (2005). Intergenerational relationships and partnerships in community programs: Purpose, practice and directions for research. *Journal of Community Psychology, 33*(1), 1–10.

Zimmerman, K., & London, J. (2003). Getting to go: Building organizational capacity to engage in youth-led research, evaluation, and planning. *CYD Journal, 4*(1), 19–25.

INDEX

NOTES

NOTES

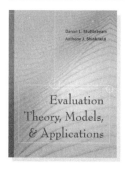

Evaluation Theory, Models, and Applications
Daniel L. Stufflebeam, Anthony J. Shinkfield

Hardcover, 768 pages
ISBN: 978-0-7879-7765-8

Evaluation Theory, Models, and Applications is a comprehensive resource designed to help evaluators and students develop a commanding knowledge of the evaluation field: its history, theory and standards, models and approaches, procedures, and inclusion of personnel and program evaluation. This important book shows how to choose from the growing array of program evaluation approaches.

The authors have compiled vital information from the evaluation literature and draw on a wide range of practical experience. Using this book, evaluators will be able to identify, analyze, and judge 26 evaluation approaches and to apply the Joint Committee Program Evaluation Standards to discriminate between legitimate and illicit approaches.

Evaluation Theory, Models, and Applications is both a textbook and a handbook. It includes down-to-earth procedures, checklists, and illustrations of how to carry out a sequence of essential evaluation tasks; identify and assess evaluation opportunities; prepare an institution to support a projected evaluation; design, budget, and contract evaluations; collect, analyze, and synthesize information; and report and facilitate use of findings. The book also addresses and illustrates metaevaluation, the fundamental process by which evaluators hold themselves accountable for delivering evaluation services that are useful, practical, ethical, and technically sound. Review exercises and group discussion questions reinforce readers' understanding of the material.

Daniel L. Stufflebeam, Ph.D., is Distinguished University Professor and Harold and Beulah McKee Professor of Education at Western Michigan University, Kalamazoo. He founded the Evaluation Center at Ohio State University in 1965 and was its director until 2002.

Anthony J. Shinkfield, Ed.D., has served in numerous positions in education leadership, including assistant director, Research and Planning Directorate, Education Department of South Australia. He is currently involved in the evaluation of independent schools and universities in Australia.

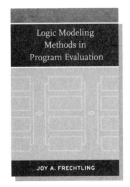

Logic Modeling Methods in Program Evaluation

Joy A. Frechtling

Paperback, 160 pages
ISBN: 978-0-7879-8196-9

"The book has plenty to hold the interest of the seasoned professional but is particularly suitable for those new to the field of evaluation. It packs the essentials."
— JAY C. THOMAS, PsycCritiques: The APA Review of Books, August, 2007.

Written for students, researchers, consultants, professionals, and scholars, *Logic Modeling Methods in Program Evaluation* provides a step-by-step explanation of logic modeling and its importance in connecting theory with implementation and outcomes in program evaluation in the social sciences.

Logic Modeling Methods in Program Evaluation is an important resource for anyone who wants to have a better understanding of the application of the logic model.

Joy A. Frechtling is a vice president and associate director in Westat's Education Studies Group. She has more than thirty years' experience in conducting educational evaluation, addressing all levels of the educational system.

Mixed Methods in Social Inquiry
Jennifer C. Greene

Paperback, 232 pages
ISBN: 978-0-7879-8382-6

"An excellent addition to the literature of integrated methodology . . . The author has skillfully integrated diverse ways of thinking about mixed methods into a comprehensive and meaningful framework. She makes it easy for both the students and the practitioners to understand the intricate details and complexities of doing mixed methods research."

—ABBAS TASHAKKORI, Frost Professor and coordinator, educational research and evaluation methodology, Department of Educational and Psychological Studies, Florida International University, founding coeditor, *Journal of Mixed Methods Research*

"Jennifer Greene's 'mixed methods way of thinking' takes us beyond the mechanics of the process and toward the multifaceted understandings which only those methods can generate."

—CHARLES TEDDLIE, distinguished professor of education, Louisiana State University

"An exquisite and indispensable map for those who are ready for the challenge of genuinely mixing methods."

—MICHAEL QUINN PATTON, author, *Utilization-Focused Evaluation and Qualitative Research and Evaluation Methods*

"This is the best available book on the topic for both scholars and students."

—MARY LEE SMITH, regents professor, Arizona State University

Jennifer Greene is professor in quantitative and evaluative research methodologies, Department of Educational Psychology, College of Education, at the University of Illinois, Champaign.

Designing and Constructing Instruments for Social Research and Evaluation
David Colton, Robert W. Covert

Paperback, 412 pages
ISBN: 978-0-7879-8784-8

Designing and Constructing Instruments for Social Research and Evaluation is a comprehensive step-by-step guide to creating effective surveys, polls, questionnaires, customer satisfaction forms, ratings, checklists, and other instruments. This book can be used by both those who are developing instruments for the first time and those who want to hone their skills, including students, agency personnel, program managers, and researchers. This book provides a thorough presentation of instrument construction, from conception to development and pretesting of items, formatting the instrument, administration, and, finally, data management and presentation of the findings. Included are guidelines for reviewing and revising the questionnaire to enhance validity and reliability, and for working effectively with stakeholders such as instrument designers, decision-makers, agency personnel, clients, and raters or respondents.

David Colton, Ph.D., is adjunct professor at the University of Virginia's Curry School of Graduate Studies in the program in Research, Statistics, and Evaluation, and in the Department of Health Care Administration, Mary Baldwin College, Staunton, Virginia.

Robert W. Covert, Ph.D., is associate professor at the University of Virginia's Curry School of Graduate Studies in the program in Research, Statistics, and Evaluation.

Methods in Educational Research: From Theory to Practice
Marguerite G. Lodico, Dean T. Spaulding, Katherine H. Voegtle

Hardcover, 440 pages
ISBN: 978-0-7879-7962-1

Written for students, educators, and researchers, *Methods in Educational Research* offers a refreshing introduction to the principles of educational research. Designed for the real world of educational research, the book's approach focuses on the types of problems likely to be encountered in professional experiences. Reflecting the importance of the No Child Left Behind Act, "scientifically based" educational research, school accountability, and the professional demands of the twenty-first century, this book empowers educational researchers to take an active role in conducting research in their classrooms, districts, and the greater educational community—activities that are now not only expected but required of all teachers.

Special features in the book assist the teaching and learning processes, such as vignettes illustrating research that is tied to practice and used to make decisions about educational practices, conceptual practical aspects of conducting research, issues and concepts relevant to the accountability movement and data-driven decision making, and sample research proposals using both qualitative and quantitative approaches. Key concepts are highlighted in each chapter, and discussion questions are provided to stimulate thought about the issues raised or encourage students to apply the concepts presented.

Marguerite G. Lodico, Ed.D., is professor at The College of Saint Rose, where she teaches child development and educational research. In addition to her teaching responsibilities, she conducts research in urban schools and community settings.

Dean T. Spaulding, Ph.D., is associate professor at The College of Saint Rose, where he teaches educational research and program evaluation and conducts evaluations of school and community programs.

Katherine H. Voegtle, Ph.D., is associate professor at The College of Saint Rose, where she teaches courses in human development and educational research and conducts research on diversity and child development.